TO:

_____

FROM:

_____

DATE:

_____

# GOD'S WORDS
## OF LIFE
### *for* FATHERS

# GOD'S WORDS
## OF LIFE
### *for* FATHERS

ZONDERVAN®

*God's Words of Life for Fathers*

Copyright © 2018 by Zondervan

This title is also available as a Zondervan ebook.

Requests for information should be addressed to:

Zondervan, *3900 Sparks Dr. SE, Grand Rapids, Michigan 49546*

ISBN: 978-031-009199–8

Previously published as *God's Words of Life for Dads*.

Excerpts taken from: *The Devotional Bible for Dads, New International Version*. Copyright © 1999 by Zondervan. All rights reserved.

All devotional thoughts were written by Robert Wolgemuth.

*Printed in China*

18  19  20  21  22  DSC  10  9  8  7  6  5  4  3  2  1

*In righteousness you will be established.*

Isaiah 54:14

# Contents

# God's Words of Life on
# ANGER

Better a patient person than a warrior,

one with self-control than one who takes a city.

PROVERBS 16:32

Everyone should be quick to listen, slow to speak and slow to become angry, because human anger does not produce the righteousness that God desires.

JAMES 1:19–20

"In your anger do not sin": Do not let the sun go down while you are still angry.

EPHESIANS 4:26

Starting a quarrel is like breaching a dam;

so drop the matter before a dispute breaks out.

PROVERBS 17:14

A gentle answer turns away wrath,

but a harsh word stirs up anger.

PROVERBS 15:1

Do not take revenge, my dear friends, but leave room for God's wrath, for it is written: "It is mine to avenge; I will repay," says the Lord.

ROMANS 12:19

Do not be quickly provoked in your spirit,
    for anger resides in the lap of fools.

ECCLESIASTES 7:9

Whoever is patient has great understanding,
    but one who is quick-tempered displays folly.

PROVERBS 14:29

The wise fear the LORD and shun evil,
    but a fool is hotheaded and yet feels secure.
A quick-tempered person does foolish things,
    and the one who devises evil schemes is hated.

PROVERBS 14:16–17

A hot-tempered person stirs up conflict,
    but the one who is patient calms a quarrel.

PROVERBS 15:18

I want the men everywhere to pray, lifting up holy hands without anger or disputing.

1 TIMOTHY 2:8

Do not make friends with a hot-tempered person,
    do not associate with one easily angered,
or you may learn their ways
    and get yourself ensnared.

Proverbs 22:24–25

Love is patient, love is kind. It does not envy, it does not boast, it is not proud. It does not dishonor others, it is not self-seeking, it is not easily angered, it keeps no record of wrongs.

1 Corinthians 13:4–5

If your enemy is hungry, give him food to eat;
    if he is thirsty, give him water to drink.
In doing this, you will heap burning coals on his head,
    and the Lord will reward you.

Proverbs 25:21–22

"Anyone who is angry with a brother or sister will be subject to judgment. . . . Therefore, if you are offering your gift at the altar and there remember that your brother or sister has something against you, leave your gift there in front of the altar. First go and be reconciled to them; then come and offer your gift."

Matthew 5:22–24

*Devotional Thought on*
# ANGER

From the beginning of the account of Job and his trials, God collected Job's complaints like coupons. Then, in chapters 38 through 41, God visits the grocery store. Aisle by aisle, line by line, verse by verse, the sovereign God gets ready to cash in His coupons at Job's checkout counter. Nowhere else in the Bible does God more thoroughly defend Himself.

Taking a step back, I find the most striking thing about this monologue is neither God's outburst nor the fact of His right to defend Himself. To me, the most amazing thing is that God chooses not to do this in other places in the Bible. Instead of putting people in their rightful place when they deserve it, God more often than not is merciful and slow to anger. So God's power is not revealed in His speech to Job. Rather it's revealed in His incredible restraint.

Every time you hold back from the lecture you think your family "deserves," you add more coupons. Now, take a lesson from God's actions in the Bible. Learn the power of mercy and restraint. Cash in these coupons only when the time comes to transform that withheld power into something truly important—and helpful—to your family.

# God's Words of Life on
# COMMITMENT

❧✦❧

Let us not become weary in doing good, for at the
proper time we will reap a harvest if we do not give up.

<small>GALATIANS 6:9</small>

Be strong and do not give up, for your work will be
rewarded.

<small>2 CHRONICLES 15:7</small>

Commit your way to the LORD;
    trust in him and he will do this:
He will make your righteous reward shine like the dawn,
    your vindication like the noonday sun.

<small>PSALM 37:5–6</small>

Love does not delight in evil but rejoices with the truth.
It always protects, always trusts, always hopes, always
perseveres.

<small>1 CORINTHIANS 13:6–7</small>

"I will make an everlasting covenant with them: I will never stop doing good to them, and I will inspire them to fear me, so that they will never turn away from me."

Jeremiah 32:40

May your hearts be fully committed to the Lord our God, to live by his decrees and obey his commands.

1 Kings 8:61

Place me like a seal over your heart,
    like a seal on your arm;
for love is as strong as death.

Song of Songs 8:6

Anyone who runs ahead and does not continue in the teaching of Christ does not have God; whoever continues in the teaching has both the Father and the Son.

2 John v. 9

Lord, who may dwell in your sacred tent?
    Who may live on your holy mountain?
The one whose walk is blameless,
    who does what is righteous,
    who speaks the truth from their heart.

Psalm 15:1–2

Do not conform to the pattern of this world, but be transformed by the renewing of your mind. Then you will be able to test and approve what God's will is—his good, pleasing and perfect will.

ROMANS 12:2

"I am coming soon. Hold on to what you have, so that no one will take your crown."

REVELATION 3:11

## *Devotional Thought on*
# COMMITMENT

I knew Captain John K. Mitchell for two hours and fifty-five minutes, exactly the time it took to fly from Nashville to Phoenix. John was a naval officer, transferring to another plane in Phoenix. "Where's your wife?" I asked, having seen his wedding band.

"Oh, I lost Florence four years ago," he responded, his eyes telling me that the pain was still fresh. "During the time God gave us together, we lived by the verse 'And we know that in all things God works for the good of those who love him.' God was so good to me to give me the years I did have with Florence." John and Florence Mitchell had been married for sixty-six years. A full thirty years before her death, a stroke had mercilessly stricken her, rendering her an invalid. "I took care of her every single day," Captain Mitchell told me. "I wouldn't have had it any other way. It was my honor."

God may not work "all things" exactly according to our plans. But if we walk with our heavenly Father, if we obey His call, we will, like Captain John K. Mitchell, be able to look back and declare all things "good."

# God's Words of Life on
# COMMUNICATION

May these words of my mouth and this meditation
   of my heart
      be pleasing in your sight,
         Lord, my Rock and my Redeemer.

PSALM 19:14

From the fruit of their lips people enjoy good things.

PROVERBS 13:2

The tongue of the righteous is choice silver.

PROVERBS 10:20

The hearts of the wise make their mouths prudent,
      and their lips promote instruction.

PROVERBS 16:23

[Speak] to one another with psalms, hymns, and songs
from the Spirit. Sing and make music from your heart
to the Lord, always giving thanks to God the Father for
everything, in the name of our Lord Jesus Christ.

EPHESIANS 5:19–20

Through Jesus . . . let us continually offer to God a sacrifice of praise—the fruit of lips that openly profess his name.

Hebrews 13:15

Like apples of gold in settings of silver
    is a ruling rightly given.

Proverbs 25:11

Gracious words are a honeycomb,
    sweet to the soul and healing to the bones.

Proverbs 16:24

A person finds joy in giving an apt reply—
    and how good is a timely word!

Proverbs 15:23

The Sovereign Lord has given me a
    well-instructed tongue,
        to know the word that sustains the weary.

Isaiah 50:4

The soothing tongue is a tree of life.

Proverbs 15:4

Always be prepared to give an answer to everyone who asks you to give the reason for the hope that you have. But do this with gentleness and respect, keeping a clear conscience.

1 Peter 3:15–16

Speaking the truth in love, we will grow to become in every respect the mature body of him who is the head, that is, Christ.

Ephesians 4:15

The tongue of the wise adorns knowledge.

Proverbs 15:2

Whoever of you loves life
    and desires to see many good days,
keep your tongue from evil
    and your lips from telling lies.
Turn from evil and do good;
    seek peace and pursue it.

Psalm 34:12–14

An honest answer
    is like a kiss on the lips.

Proverbs 24:26

Let your conversation be always full of grace, seasoned with salt, so that you may know how to answer everyone.

Colossians 4:6

If anyone speaks, they should do so as one who speaks the very words of God.

1 Peter 4:11

## Devotional Thought on
# COMMUNICATION

When we were much younger, most of us heard the kids in the neighborhood chant, "Sticks and stones may break my bones, but words will never hurt me."

It's nonsense. Why? Because words are powerful.

And, at times, they can hurt deeply.

Zerubbabel and his crew were busily rebuilding the temple that once had been the center of Jewish life. Enemies of the Jews from neighboring countries tried to hurt Zerubbabel and his associates—not with fists or weapons, but with their words. They even sent in trained specialists ("officials to work against them," Ezra 4:5) to extract the enthusiasm and joy from these faithful people. Zerubbabel defended their cause and countered the cruel and discouraging words that might have weakened his people's hands.

We also have the power of these "officials": our words can frighten our children and weaken the very ones we love. But thankfully we also can choose to imitate Zerubbabel in speaking good words that will encourage our kids. We can literally reverse fearfulness and give our families strength— just with the things we say.

Choose your words carefully. They have unbelievable power.

# *God's Words of Life on* COURAGE

The Lord is my light and my salvation—
   whom shall I fear?
The Lord is the stronghold of my life—
   of whom shall I be afraid?

PSALM 27:1

"Do not fear, for I am with you;
   do not be dismayed, for I am your God."

ISAIAH 41:10

"Be strong and courageous. Do not be afraid; do not be discouraged, for the Lord your God will be with you wherever you go."

JOSHUA 1:9

Do not be anxious about anything, but in every situation, by prayer and petition, with thanksgiving, present your requests to God. And the peace of God, which transcends all understanding, will guard your hearts and your minds in Christ Jesus.

PHILIPPIANS 4:6–7

I can do all this through him who gives me strength.

Philippians 4:13

Dear friends, do not be surprised at the fiery ordeal
that has come on you to test you, as though something
strange were happening to you. But rejoice inasmuch as
you participate in the sufferings of Christ, so that you
may be overjoyed when his glory is revealed.

1 Peter 4:12–13

"When you pass through the waters,
    I will be with you;
and when you pass through the rivers,
    they will not sweep over you.
When you walk through the fire,
    you will not be burned;
    the flames will not set you ablaze."

Isaiah 43:2

Strengthen the feeble hands,
    steady the knees that give way;
say to those with fearful hearts,
    "Be strong, do not fear;
your God will come,
    he will come with vengeance."

Isaiah 35:3–4

In all these things we are more than conquerors through him who loved us. For I am convinced that neither death nor life, neither angels nor demons, neither the present nor the future, nor any powers, neither height nor depth, nor anything else in all creation, will be able to separate us from the love of God that is in Christ Jesus our Lord.

ROMANS 8:37–39

Wait for the LORD;
> be strong and take heart
> and wait for the LORD.

PSALM 27:14

He gives strength to the weary
> and increases the power of the weak.
Even youths grow tired and weary,
> and young men stumble and fall;
but those who hope in the LORD
> will renew their strength.
They will soar on wings like eagles;
> they will run and not grow weary,
> they will walk and not be faint.

ISAIAH 40:29–31

*Devotional Thought on*
# COURAGE

A small bookcase stood behind the overstuffed chair in the corner of my parents' living room. One of the volumes in that case was a huge book titled *Foxe's Book of Martyrs*. The tome was filled with actual accounts of individuals who, because of their love for Jesus Christ, were willing to die for Him. I can vividly remember sitting on the floor behind that chair. Slowly I would turn the pages, my eyes fixed on the graphic drawings of how these incredibly courageous men and women gladly endured the most grisly torture imaginable instead of denying their loyalty and love for their Savior.

Although worldwide persecution of Christians continues today, it's safe to say that our defense of our Savior will probably never be as severe as these. But we are—and will be constantly—challenged to compromise what's right. Even today we may find ourselves looking at tempting circumstances and intimidating accusers. Although our loyalty to Jesus Christ may cost us, it will always be rewarding.

I love to envision Stephen the martyr (Acts 7) and Jesus meeting in heaven. "Thank you," Jesus must have said to His loyal friend. "You're welcome," Stephen may have replied, "but You did it for me."

# God's Words of Life on
# DECISIONS

Counsel and sound judgment are mine;
    I have insight, I have power. . . .
I love those who love me,
    and those who seek me find me.

PROVERBS 8:14, 17

The heart of the discerning acquires knowledge,
    for the ears of the wise seek it out.

PROVERBS 18:15

If any of you lacks wisdom, he should ask God, who gives
generously to all without finding fault, and it will be given
to you. But when you ask, you must believe and not doubt,
because the one who doubts is like a wave of the sea,
blown and tossed by the wind.

JAMES 1:5–6

Help us, God our Savior,
    for the glory of your name.

PSALM 79:9

Trust in the LORD with all your heart
    and lean not on your own understanding;
in all your ways submit to him,
    and he will make your paths straight.

PROVERBS 3:5–6

The LORD confides in those who fear him;
    he makes his covenant known to them.

PSALM 25:14

It is God who works in you to will and to act in order to fulfill his good purpose.

PHILIPPIANS 2:13

Plans are established by seeking advice.

PROVERBS 20:18

Direct me in the path of your commands,
    for there I find delight.

PSALM 119:35

The Spirit of truth . . . will guide you into all the truth. He will not speak on his own; he will speak only what he hears, and he will tell you what is yet to come.

JOHN 16:13

"The LORD will guide you always."

ISAIAH 58:11

I instruct you in the way of wisdom
and lead you along straight paths.

PROVERBS 4:11

Direct my footsteps according to your word.

PSALM 119:133

Teach me to do your will,
for you are my God;
may your good Spirit
lead me on level ground.

PSALM 143:10

Since you are my rock and my fortress,
for the sake of your name lead and guide me.

PSALM 31:3

In your unfailing love you will lead
the people you have redeemed.

EXODUS 15:13

"Do not let your hearts be troubled. You believe in God;
believe also in me."

JOHN 14:1

Show me the way I should go,
for to you I entrust my life.

PSALM 143:8

Let the one who walks in the dark,
   who has no light,
trust in the name of the LORD
   and rely on their God.

ISAIAH 50:10

In their hearts humans plan their course,
   but the LORD establishes their steps.

PROVERBS 16:9

"I will instruct you and teach you in the way you should go;
   I will counsel you with my loving eye on you."

PSALM 32:8

Listen to advice and accept discipline,
   and at the end you will be counted among the wise.

PROVERBS 19:20

This is the confidence we have in approaching God: that if we ask anything according to his will, he hears us.

1 JOHN 5:14

You have known the Holy Scriptures, which are able to make you wise for salvation through faith in Christ Jesus.

2 TIMOTHY 3:15

Give your servant a discerning heart to govern your
people and to distinguish between right and wrong.

1 Kings 3:9

Get wisdom, get understanding;
        do not forget my words or turn away from them.
Do not forsake wisdom, and she will protect you;
        love her, and she will watch over you.
The beginning of wisdom is this: Get wisdom.
        Though it cost all you have, get understanding.

Proverbs 4:5–7

Your word is a lamp for my feet,
        a light on my path.

Psalm 119:105

The way of fools seems right to them,
        but the wise listen to advice.

Proverbs 12:15

Show me your ways, Lord,
        teach me your paths.
Guide me in your truth and teach me,
        for you are God my Savior,
        and my hope is in you all day long.

Psalm 25:4–5

*Devotional Thought on*

# DECISIONS

Being a good dad is a very tough job. Given a choice, every dad would prefer being liked by his family to not being liked. Unfortunately, there are many times in the lives of families when the dad would come in dead last on his kids' "Dad of the Year" nominee list. Leadership can be like that.

Poor Moses knew something about this. He had just been personally responsible for the release of over two million Jews from captivity—no small job. But now these people were being squeezed between the Red Sea and the entire Egyptian army. And they were very upset at Moses.

So Moses gave them a little talk, telling them not to be afraid, to hold steady, and to watch God do this thing. Given what looked like the ultimate rock and a hard place, how could he possibly have been so sure? The answer lies in the chapters leading up to this amazing story. Moses had kept in close contact with the Lord. His assurance came from God Himself.

The secret to your success as a dad doesn't depend on how pleased your children are with your decisions. The key is in who is calling the shots for you.

# God's Words of Life on
# DIFFICULT TIMES

"In this world you will have trouble. But take heart!
I have overcome the world."

John 16:33

But [God] knows the way that I take;
   when he has tested me, I will come forth as gold.

Job 23:10

Join with me in suffering, like a good soldier of Christ Jesus.

2 Timothy 2:3

It has been granted to you on behalf of Christ not only
to believe in him, but also to suffer for him.

Philippians 1:29

He was despised and rejected by mankind,
   a man of suffering, and familiar with pain.

Isaiah 53:3

Just as we share abundantly in the sufferings of Christ,
so also our comfort abounds through Christ.

2 Corinthians 1:5

The LORD disciplines those he loves.

PROVERBS 3:12

Our present sufferings are not worth comparing with
the glory that will be revealed in us.

ROMANS 8:18

If you are insulted because of the name of Christ, you are
blessed, for the Spirit of glory and of God rests on you.

1 PETER 4:14

We . . . glory in our sufferings, because we know that
suffering produces perseverance; perseverance, character;
and character, hope.

ROMANS 5:3–4

Consider it pure joy . . . whenever you face trials of many
kinds, because you know that the testing of your faith
develops perseverance.

JAMES 1:2–3

[The Lord] has not despised or scorned
    the suffering of the afflicted one;
he has not hidden his face from him
    but has listened to his cry for help.

PSALM 22:24

For Christ's sake, I delight in weaknesses, in insults, in hardships, in persecutions, in difficulties. For when I am weak, then I am strong.

2 Corinthians 12:10

The righteous person may have many troubles,
    but the Lord delivers him from them all.

Psalm 34:19

Blessed is the one who perseveres under trial because, having stood the test, that person will receive the crown of life that the Lord has promised to those who love him.

James 1:12

Because he himself suffered when he was tempted, [Jesus] is able to help those who are being tempted.

Hebrews 2:18

When I called, you answered me;
    you greatly emboldened me.

Psalm 138:3

The Spirit helps us in our weakness. We do not know what we ought to pray for, but the Spirit himself intercedes for us through wordless groans.

Romans 8:26

Our struggle is not against flesh and blood, but against the rulers, against the authorities, against the powers of this dark world and against the spiritual forces of evil in the heavenly realms.

Ephesians 6:12

Fight the good fight of the faith. Take hold of the eternal life to which you were called.

1 Timothy 6:12

Let the beloved of the Lord rest secure in him,
> for he shields him all day long,
> and the one the Lord loves rests between his shoulders.

Deuteronomy 33:12

In the day of trouble
> [the Lord] will keep me safe in his dwelling;
he will hide me in the shelter of his sacred tent
> and set me high upon a rock.

Psalm 27:5

You have been my refuge,
> a strong tower against the foe.
I long to dwell in your tent forever
> and take refuge in the shelter of your wings.

Psalm 61:3–4

Whoever dwells in the shelter of the Most High
  will rest in the shadow of the Almighty.

Psalm 91:1

You have been a refuge for the poor,
  a refuge for the needy in their distress,
a shelter from the storm
  and a shade from the heat.

Isaiah 25:4

We wait in hope for the Lord;
  he is our help and our shield.

Psalm 33:20

No discipline seems pleasant at the time, but painful.
Later on, however, it produces a harvest of righteousness
and peace for those who have been trained by it.

Hebrews 12:11

Those who sow with tears
  will reap with songs of joy.
Those who go out weeping,
  carrying seed to sow,
will return with songs of joy,
  carrying sheaves with them.

Psalm 126:5–6

## Devotional Thought on
# DIFFICULT TIMES

I read the story of the disciples challenging Jesus with a tough question about a blind man. "Who sinned, this man or his parents?" (John 9:2). When His disciples asked this question, Jesus answered, "This happened so that the works of God might be displayed in him" (John 9:3).

You and I may live our lives with our eyesight intact. But we're going to experience pain, loss, doubt, and grief. We will find ourselves questioning God's judgment in allowing us to be so severely set back. During those times, we need to remember that God's purposes are always the same. He acts, He moves, He decides our futures based on our circumstances' ability to deliver praise to His holy name.

Jesus healed the blind man. He may heal us or restore our net worth . . . or not. But regardless, our task is—and will always be—to rest in His grace. Our charge is to take comfort that, though we may be in the midst of darkness, He is the Light of the World.

Thank God for the pain. It provides for us the privilege of seeing and glorifying Him.

# *God's Words of Life on* ENCOURAGEMENT

"In this world you will have trouble. But take heart!
I have overcome the world."

JOHN 16:33

[God's] mercy extends to those who fear him,
from generation to generation.

LUKE 1:50

Yet this I call to mind
and therefore I have hope:
Because of the LORD's great love we are not consumed,
for his compassions never fail.
They are new every morning;
great is your faithfulness.

LAMENTATIONS 3:21–23

Cast your cares on the LORD
and he will sustain you;
he will never let
the righteous be shaken.

PSALM 55:22

29

Cast all your anxiety on him because he cares for you.

1 Peter 5:7

In my alarm I said,
    "I am cut off from your sight!"
Yet you heard my cry for mercy
    when I called to you for help. . . .
Be strong and take heart,
    all you who hope in the Lord.

Psalm 31:22, 24

Let the morning bring me word of your unfailing love,
    for I have put my trust in you.

Psalm 143:8

The Lord is a refuge for the oppressed,
    a stronghold in times of trouble.

Psalm 9:9

Why, my soul, are you downcast?
    Why so disturbed within me?
Put your hope in God,
    for I will yet praise him,
    my Savior and my God.

Psalm 42:5

The eternal God is your refuge,

and underneath are the everlasting arms.

Deuteronomy 33:27

God is our refuge and strength,

an ever-present help in trouble.

Therefore we will not fear, though the earth give way

and the mountains fall into the heart of the sea,

though its waters roar and foam

and the mountains quake with their surging.

Psalm 46:1–3

I sought the Lord, and he answered me;

he delivered me from all my fears.

Psalm 34:4

Truly my soul finds rest in God;

my salvation comes from him.

Truly he is my rock and my salvation;

he is my fortress, I will never be shaken.

Psalm 62:1–2

When I said, "My foot is slipping,"

your unfailing love, Lord, supported me.

When anxiety was great within me,

your consolation brought me joy.

Psalm 94:18–19

The LORD upholds all who fall
and lifts up all who are bowed down.

"I am the LORD your God
who takes hold of your right hand
and says to you, Do not fear;
I will help you."

ISAIAH 41:13

In all their distress [the LORD] too was distressed,
and the angel of his presence saved them.
In his love and mercy he redeemed them;
he lifted them up and carried them
all the days of old.

ISAIAH 63:9

"Come to me, all you who are weary and burdened, and
I will give you rest. Take my yoke upon you and learn
from me, for I am gentle and humble in heart, and you
will find rest for your souls."

MATTHEW 11:28–29

"I will refresh the weary and satisfy the faint."

JEREMIAH 31:25

"My grace is sufficient for you, for my power is made
perfect in weakness."

2 Corinthians 12:9

You are my hiding place;
>   you will protect me from trouble
>   and surround me with songs of deliverance.

Psalm 32:7

Though I have fallen, I will rise.
Though I sit in darkness,
>   the Lord will be my light.

Micah 7:8

God is faithful, who has called you into fellowship with
his Son, Jesus Christ our Lord.

1 Corinthians 1:9

The Lord is good to those whose hope is in him,
>   to the one who seeks him.

Lamentations 3:25

Whatever is true, whatever is noble, whatever is
right, whatever is pure, whatever is lovely, whatever is
admirable—if anything is excellent or praiseworthy—
think about such things.

Philippians 4:8

## Devotional Thought on
# ENCOURAGEMENT

If you were to drive past the football practice field just behind our local high school, you would see a wooden tower standing probably eighteen to twenty feet in the air. My guess is that very few people have any idea what it's for.

But you know, don't you? It's for the coaches during practice. Climbing up to the raised platform gives them a different look at various plays and strategies. It gives them perspective—something that can be a lot more difficult standing at ground level.

Joseph was despised by his brothers, sold like a dog, and thrown into prison on a bum rap. But God helped Joseph to "look down" on these events and realize that, in God's sovereign mercy, each had happened for his own good and for the survival of his family. Now there's a panoramic look.

What has happened to you and your family that makes you wonder if God knows what He's doing? Are you on the field, squashed by a 350-pound linebacker and trying to figure out what's going on, or are you in the tower of God's perspective?

Ask Him to lift you up. He's the very same God who lifted Joseph, and He'll do it for you.

# God's Words of Life on
# FAILURE

We do not have a high priest who is unable to empathize with our weaknesses, but we have one who has been tempted in every way, just as we are—yet he did not sin. Let us then approach God's throne of grace with confidence, so that we may receive mercy and find grace to help us in our time of need.

HEBREWS 4:15–16

The LORD God . . . is with you. He will not fail you or forsake you.

1 CHRONICLES 28:20

Plans fail for lack of counsel,
    but with many advisers they succeed.

PROVERBS 15:22

If we are faithless,
    [Christ] remains faithful,
    for he cannot disown himself.

2 TIMOTHY 2:13

The Lord is good,
>
> a refuge in times of trouble.

He cares for those who trust in him.

NAHUM 1:7

Though I walk in the midst of trouble,
>
> you preserve my life.

You stretch out your hand against the anger of my foes;
>
> with your right hand you save me.

PSALM 138:7

We know that in all things God works for the good of those who love him, who have been called according to his purpose.

ROMANS 8:28

I lift up my eyes to the mountains—
>
> where does my help come from?

My help comes from the LORD,
>
> the Maker of heaven and earth.

PSALM 121:1–2

Stand firm. Let nothing move you. Always give yourselves fully to the work of the Lord, because you know that your labor in the Lord is not in vain.

1 CORINTHIANS 15:58

Praise be to the God and Father of our Lord Jesus Christ, the Father of compassion and the God of all comfort, who comforts us in all our troubles, so that we can comfort those in any trouble with the comfort we ourselves receive from God.

2 CORINTHIANS 1:3–4

I said, "I have labored in vain;
    I have spent my strength for nothing at all.
Yet what is due me is in the LORD's hand,
    and my reward is with my God."

ISAIAH 49:4

## *Devotional Thought on*
# FAILURE

Many dads struggle with life. Sometimes things from their pasts can literally disable men. In some cases, these awful circumstances have become the reason why they have given up on life . . . or have tragically failed.

Jesus was on His way to the temple feast when He passed a pool called *Bethesda*—the word means "a place of kindness." Tradition had it that when the water in this pool began to stir, the first person to touch it would be healed. There Jesus encountered a disabled man. As He did so often in working miracles of healing, Jesus changed this man's perspective, then He healed him . . . heaping kindness upon kindness.

Have you been "disabled" by some past event in your life? Have you allowed this event to darken your past, hamper your present, and cast doubt on your future? If so, are you ready for Jesus' brand of kindness? Allow Him to give you the will to heal your yesterday and lavish you with wholeness for tomorrow.

# God's Words of Life on
# FAITH

Faith is confidence in what we hope for and
assurance about what we do not see.

Hebrews 11:1

Make every effort to add to your faith goodness; and to
goodness, knowledge; and to knowledge, self-control;
and to self-control, perseverance; and to perseverance,
godliness; and to godliness, mutual affection; and to
mutual affection, love.

2 Peter 1:5–7

Faith comes from hearing the message, and the message
is heard through the word about Christ.

Romans 10:17

[Let us fix] our eyes on Jesus, the pioneer and perfecter
of faith. For the joy set before him he endured the cross,
scorning its shame, and sat down at the right hand of the
throne of God.

Hebrews 12:2

Abram believed the LORD, and he credited it to him as righteousness.

GENESIS 15:6

"Have faith in God," Jesus answered. "Truly I tell you, if anyone says to this mountain, 'Go, throw yourself into the sea,' and does not doubt in their heart but believes that what they say will happen, it will be done for them. Therefore I tell you, whatever you ask for in prayer, believe that you have received it, and it will be yours."

MARK 11:22–24

In the gospel the righteousness of God is revealed—a righteousness that is by faith from first to last, just as it is written: "The righteous will live by faith."

ROMANS 1:17

We live by faith, not by sight.

2 CORINTHIANS 5:7

By faith even Sarah, who was past childbearing age, was enabled to bear children because she considered him faithful who had made the promise.

HEBREWS 11:11

Without faith it is impossible to please God.

HEBREWS 11:6

[Trials] have come so that the proven genuineness of your faith—of greater worth than gold, which perishes even though refined by fire—may result in praise, glory and honor when Jesus Christ is revealed.

1 PETER 1:7

By faith we understand that the universe was formed at God's command, so that what is seen was not made out of what was visible.

HEBREWS 11:3

In his great mercy [God] has given us new birth into a living hope through the resurrection of Jesus Christ from the dead, and into an inheritance that can never perish, spoil or fade. This inheritance is kept in heaven for you, who through faith are shielded by God's power until the coming of the salvation that is ready to be revealed in the last time.

1 PETER 1:3–5

By faith Moses, when he had grown up, refused to be known as the son of Pharaoh's daughter. He chose to be mistreated along with the people of God rather than to enjoy the fleeting pleasures of sin. He regarded disgrace for the sake of Christ as of greater value than the treasures of Egypt, because he was looking ahead to his reward.

HEBREWS 11:24–26

To all who did receive [Christ], to those who believed in his name, he gave the right to become children of God— children born not of natural descent, nor of human decision or a husband's will, but born of God.

JOHN 1:12–13

Since we have been justified through faith, we have peace with God through our Lord Jesus Christ.

ROMANS 5:1

It is by grace you have been saved, through faith—and this is not from yourselves, it is the gift of God—not by works, so that no one can boast.

EPHESIANS 2:8–9

"My Father's will is that everyone who looks to the Son and believes in him shall have eternal life, and I will raise them up at the last day."

JOHN 6:40

Righteousness is given through faith in Jesus Christ to all who believe. There is no difference between Jew and Gentile, for all have sinned and fall short of the glory of God, and all are justified freely by his grace through the redemption that came by Christ Jesus.

ROMANS 3:22–24

"God did not send his Son into the world to condemn the world, but to save the world through him. Whoever believes in him is not condemned."

JOHN 3:17–18

"Very truly I tell you, whoever hears my word and believes him who sent me has eternal life and will not be judged but has crossed over from death to life."

JOHN 5:24

It was not through the law that Abraham and his offspring received the promise that he would be heir of the world, but through the righteousness that comes by faith. . . . The promise comes by faith, so that it may be by grace and may be guaranteed.

ROMANS 4:13, 16

*Devotional Thought on*
# FAITH

Jairus grieved over his daughter's pain and pleaded with Jesus to heal her. Jesus was delayed after this request, and in the meantime several men came to Jairus with terrible news for him. This daddy's girl was dead. Jairus was numb with grief.

Notice, however, Jesus' response in Mark 5:36. He didn't say anything about the dead girl. His first words were not a reassurance that the child was going to be all right. No, instead Jesus looked at this father and offered him the most incredible advice known to mankind: "Don't be afraid; just believe." Because you have read the whole story, you know that it has a happy—and absolutely miraculous—ending.

Jesus has some very sound advice for us hand-wringing fathers. He offers a bit of solace as we contemplate the need to care for and protect our children: "Don't be afraid; just believe."

*Thank You, Heavenly Father.*
*I really needed that today.*

# God's Words of Life on
# FAITHFULNESS

The LORD rewards everyone for their righteousness and faithfulness.

1 SAMUEL 26:23

Dear friend, you are faithful in what you are doing for the brothers and sisters, even though they are strangers to you.

3 JOHN v. 5

It is required that those who have been given a trust must prove faithful.

1 CORINTHIANS 4:2

They could find no corruption in [Daniel], because he was trustworthy and neither corrupt nor negligent.

DANIEL 6:4

I will praise you with the harp
    for your faithfulness, my God;
I will sing praise to you.

PSALM 71:22

"His master replied, 'Well done, good and faithful servant! You have been faithful with a few things; I will put you in charge of many things. Come and share your master's happiness!'"

MATTHEW 25:21

A faithful person will be richly blessed.

PROVERBS 28:20

I have kept the ways of the LORD;
　　I am not guilty of turning from my God.
All his laws are before me;
　　I have not turned away from his decrees.
I have been blameless before him
　　and have kept myself from sin.
The LORD has rewarded me according to my righteousness,
　　according to my cleanness in his sight.
To the faithful you show yourself faithful,
　　to the blameless you show yourself blameless.

2 SAMUEL 22:22–26

Righteousness and justice are the foundation of your
　　throne;
　　love and faithfulness go before you.
Blessed are those who . . .
　　walk in the light of your presence, LORD.

PSALM 89:14–15

May the LORD now show you kindness and faithfulness.

Your love, LORD, reaches to the heavens,
    your faithfulness to the skies.

PSALM 36:5

Great is his love toward us,
    and the faithfulness of the LORD endures forever.
Praise the LORD.

PSALM 117:2

LORD, you are my God;
    I will exalt you and praise your name,
for in perfect faithfulness
    you have done wonderful things,
    things planned long ago.

ISAIAH 25:1

"I, the LORD, love justice. . . .
In my faithfulness I will reward my people
    and make an everlasting covenant with them."

ISAIAH 61:8

It gave me great joy when some believers came and
testified about your faithfulness to the truth, telling how
you continue to walk in it.

3 JOHN v. 3

[The Lord] will cover you with his feathers,
and under his wings you will find refuge;
his faithfulness will be your shield and rampart.

PSALM 91:4

The works of [God's] hands are faithful and just;
all his precepts are trustworthy.
They are established for ever and ever,
enacted in faithfulness and uprightness.

PSALM 111:7–8

I will bow down toward your holy temple
and will praise your name
for your unfailing love and your faithfulness,
for you have so exalted your solemn decree
that it surpasses your fame.

PSALM 138:2

The fruit of the Spirit is love, joy, peace, forbearance, kindness, goodness, faithfulness, gentleness and self-control.

GALATIANS 5:22–23

Let love and faithfulness never leave you;
bind them around your neck,
write them on the tablet of your heart.

PROVERBS 3:3

The living, the living—they praise you,
   as I am doing today;
parents tell their children
   about your faithfulness.

ISAIAH 38:19

## Devotional Thought on
# FAITHFULNESS

Jesus called twelve men to follow Him. Very little is said about what these men left behind, but here were a dozen men who must have wondered about their sanity as they left everything that was comfortable, familiar, and safe to follow Jesus. With laser-beam clarity, the Master had taken aim at their wondering souls.

Choosing to be God's man in your home, in your town, or in your workplace may not earn you any immediate or visible commissions. You may experience rejection, alienation, and loneliness because of this decision. There will be times when you wonder if you've done the right thing. But Jesus' promise to you and me is certain: what we see today isn't all there is.

Someday, because of this partnership with our Savior, we will "rejoice . . . and leap for joy" (Luke 6:23). Many people have gone before us; they experienced this same uncertainty, and because they are with their heavenly Father today, their satisfaction is complete . . . for all of eternity.

# God's Words of Life on
# FATHERHOOD

We have all had human fathers who disciplined
us and we respected them for it. How much more
should we submit to the Father of spirits and
live! They disciplined us for a little while as they
thought best; but God disciplines us for our good,
in order that we may share in his holiness.

HEBREWS 12:9–10

When we were underage, we were in slavery under the
elemental spiritual forces of the world. But when the
set time had fully come, God sent his Son, born of a
woman, born under the law, to redeem those under the
law, that we might receive adoption to sonship. Because
you are his sons, God sent the Spirit of his Son into our
hearts, the Spirit who calls out, "*Abba*, Father." So you
are no longer a slave, but God's child; and since you are
his child, God has made you also an heir.

GALATIANS 4:3–7

You know that we dealt with each of you as a father deals with his own children, encouraging, comforting and urging you to live lives worthy of God, who calls you into his kingdom and glory.

1 THESSALONIANS 2:11–12

Fathers, do not exasperate your children; instead, bring them up in the training and instruction of the Lord.

EPHESIANS 6:4

"Which of you fathers, if your son asks for a fish, will give him a snake instead? Or if he asks for an egg, will give him a scorpion? If you then, though you are evil, know how to give good gifts to your children, how much more will your Father in heaven give the Holy Spirit to those who ask him!"

LUKE 11:11–13

I was young and now I am old,
    yet I have never seen the righteous forsaken
    or their children begging bread.
They are always generous and lend freely;
    their children will be a blessing.

PSALM 37:25–26

Love the LORD your God with all your heart and with all your soul and with all your strength. These commandments that I give you today are to be on your hearts. Impress them on your children. Talk about them when you sit at home and when you walk along the road, when you lie down and when you get up. Tie them as symbols on your hands and bind them on your foreheads. Write them on the doorframes of your houses and on your gates.

DEUTERONOMY 6:5–9

I will open my mouth with a parable;
　　I will utter hidden things, things from of old—
things we have heard and known,
　　things our ancestors have told us.
We will not hide them from their descendants;
　　we will tell the next generation
the praiseworthy deeds of the LORD,
　　his power, and the wonders he has done.

PSALM 78:2–4

As we have opportunity, let us do good to all people, especially to those who belong to the family of believers.

GALATIANS 6:10

*Devotional Thought on*
## FATHERHOOD

The first chapter of Genesis contains the story of creation. Almighty God literally took nothingness and made something of it with the sound of His voice. He did what He did, He took a good look, and He was pleased. Interestingly enough, the rest of the Bible confirms that God kept looking, day after day. He paid attention.

Most dads will readily admit that they have a lot to learn. This is a whole new experience for us—something our formal education didn't include. So we learn as we go. We discover what works and what doesn't. But given God's example, we should rarely catch ourselves saying, "You know, I never saw it coming," "When did she start doing that?" or "I guess I just wasn't paying attention."

Our challenge is not just to live with our families but to really be there. To understand our job as the dad is to see what's going on—to not succumb to the temptation of getting on to the next thing without continuing to watch.

God's pattern was to create, to see, and to celebrate. That's a pretty good model to follow.

# God's Words of Life on
# FEAR

The LORD is my light and my salvation—
    whom shall I fear?
The LORD is the stronghold of my life—
    of whom shall I be afraid?

PSALM 27:1

[God] will command his angels concerning you
    to guard you in all your ways;
they will lift you up in their hands,
    so that you will not strike your foot against a stone.
You will tread on the lion and the cobra;
    you will trample the great lion and the serpent.
"Because he loves me," says the LORD, "I will rescue him;
    I will protect him, for he acknowledges my name."

PSALM 91:11–14

The Spirit you received does not make you slaves, so
that you live in fear again; rather, the Spirit you received
brought about your adoption to sonship.

ROMANS 8:15

The Spirit God gave us does not make us timid, but gives us power.

2 TIMOTHY 1:7

"Do not be dismayed, for I am your God.
I will strengthen you and help you."

ISAIAH 41:10

"Do not be afraid, little flock, for your Father has been pleased to give you the kingdom."

LUKE 12:32

The Lord is my helper; I will not be afraid.

HEBREWS 13:6

When the servant of the man of God got up and went out early the next morning, an army with horses and chariots had surrounded the city. "Oh no, my lord! What shall we do?" the servant asked.

"Don't be afraid," the prophet answered. "Those who are with us are more than those who are with them."

And Elisha prayed, "Open his eyes, LORD, so that he may see." Then the LORD opened the servant's eyes, and he looked and saw the hills full of horses and chariots of fire all around Elisha.

2 KINGS 6:15–17

There is no fear in love. But perfect love drives out fear.

1 JOHN 4:18

When you lie down, you will not be afraid;
when you lie down, your sleep will be sweet.
Have no fear of sudden disaster
or of the ruin that overtakes the wicked,
for the LORD will be at your side
and will keep your foot from being snared.

PROVERBS 3:24–26

Who shall separate us from the love of Christ? Shall trouble or hardship or persecution or famine or nakedness or danger or sword? . . . No, in all these things we are more than conquerors through him who loved us.

ROMANS 8:35, 37

Be strong and courageous. Do not be afraid; do not be discouraged, for the LORD your God will be with you wherever you go.

JOSHUA 1:9

God is our refuge and strength,
an ever-present help in trouble.
Therefore we will not fear, though the earth give way
and the mountains fall into the heart of the sea.

PSALM 46:1–2

My flesh and my heart may fail,
>   but God is the strength of my heart
>   and my portion forever.

PSALM 73:26

Stand firm and you will see the deliverance the LORD will bring you today.

EXODUS 14:13

In righteousness you will be established:
>   Tyranny will be far from you;
>       you will have nothing to fear.
>   Terror will be far removed;
>       it will not come near you.

ISAIAH 54:14

Though an army besiege me,
>   my heart will not fear;
> though war break out against me,
>   even then I will be confident.

PSALM 27:3

Even though I walk
>   through the darkest valley,
> I will fear no evil.

PSALM 23:4

If God is for us, who can be against us?

Romans 8:31

The Lord is with me; I will not be afraid.

Psalm 118:6

When I am afraid, I put my trust in you.

Psalm 56:3

We were harassed at every turn—conflicts on the outside, fears within. But God, who comforts the downcast, comforted us.

2 Corinthians 7:5–6

## Devotional Thought on
# FEAR

Daniel was courageous because he had been obedient to God all along—both in the small things and in the big things. If he hadn't trained himself to obey God every day by always telling the truth, doing his job well, and treating others with kindness, he probably would have buckled when he heard the king's decree not to worship anyone but him. He probably would have thought, *God will understand if I don't pray to Him just this time. It's only for thirty days.*

But Daniel refused to dishonor God. After all, he had seen God rescue Shadrach, Meshach, and Abednego from the fiery furnace. Daniel knew that God cared about him, and he knew that God takes care of His children. So he faced what could have been his death with courage. And how did God repay him? He sent an angel to close those lions' mouths.

The same God who protected Daniel from the lions is working in our lives today. So when trouble strikes, do what Daniel did: "He got down on his knees and prayed, giving thanks to his God, just as he had done before" (Daniel 6:10).

# God's Words of Life on
# FORGIVENESS

Blessed are those

> whose transgressions are forgiven,

> whose sins are covered.

Blessed is the one

> whose sin the Lord will never count against them.

ROMANS 4:7–8

When you stand praying, if you hold anything against anyone, forgive them, so that your Father in heaven may forgive you your sins.

MARK 11:25

As far as the east is from the west,

> so far has [God] removed our transgressions from us.

PSALM 103:12

Bear with each other and forgive one another if any of you has a grievance against someone. Forgive as the Lord forgave you.

COLOSSIANS 3:13

When you were dead in your sins . . . , God made you alive with Christ. He forgave us all our sins, having canceled the charge of our legal indebtedness, which stood against us and condemned us; he has taken it away, nailing it to the cross.

COLOSSIANS 2:13–14

"Come now, let us settle the matter,"
    says the LORD.
"Though your sins are like scarlet,
    they shall be as white as snow;
though they are red as crimson,
    they shall be like wool."

ISAIAH 1:18

In him we have redemption through his blood, the forgiveness of sins, in accordance with the riches of God's grace that he lavished on us.

EPHESIANS 1:7–8

[God] has rescued us from the dominion of darkness and brought us into the kingdom of the Son he loves.

COLOSSIANS 1:13

You, Lord, are forgiving and good,
    abounding in love to all who call to you.

PSALM 86:5

The Lord our God is merciful and forgiving, even
though we have rebelled against him.

DANIEL 9:9

Who is a God like you,
> who pardons sin and forgives the transgression
> of the remnant of his inheritance?
You do not stay angry forever
> but delight to show mercy.

MICAH 7:18

Repent and be baptized, every one of you, in the name
of Jesus Christ for the forgiveness of your sins. And you
will receive the gift of the Holy Spirit. The promise is for
you and your children and for all who are far off—for all
whom the Lord our God will call.

ACTS 2:38–39

The LORD is slow to anger, abounding in love and
forgiving sin and rebellion.

NUMBERS 14:18

Forgive all our sins
> and receive us graciously,
that we may offer the fruit of our lips.

HOSEA 14:2

"Forgive us our debts,
   as we also have forgiven our debtors.
And lead us not into temptation,
   but deliver us from the evil one."

MATTHEW 6:12–13

Praise be to the Lord, the God of Israel,
   because he has come to his people and
      redeemed them.

LUKE 1:68

When the set time had fully come, God sent his Son,
born of a woman, born under the law, to redeem those
under the law, that we might receive adoption to sonship.

GALATIANS 4:4–5

Whoever conceals their sins does not prosper,
   but the one who confesses and renounces them
      finds mercy.

PROVERBS 28:13

Return to the LORD your God,
   for he is gracious and compassionate,
slow to anger and abounding in love,
   and he relents from sending calamity.

JOEL 2:13

When we were overwhelmed by sins,
you forgave our transgressions.

PSALM 65:3

"If you forgive other people when they sin against you,
your heavenly Father will also forgive you."

MATTHEW 6:14

In Christ God forgave you.

EPHESIANS 4:32

"If your brother or sister sins against you, rebuke them;
and if they repent, forgive them. Even if they sin against
you seven times in a day and seven times come back to
you saying 'I repent,' you must forgive them."

LUKE 17:3–4

"If my people, who are called by my name, will humble
themselves and pray and seek my face and turn from
their wicked ways, then I will hear from heaven, and I
will forgive their sin and will heal their land."

2 CHRONICLES 7:14

Wash away all my iniquity
and cleanse me from my sin.

PSALM 51:2

You are a forgiving God, gracious and compassionate, slow to anger and abounding in love.

NEHEMIAH 9:17

God was pleased to have all his fullness dwell in [Christ], and through him to reconcile to himself all things, whether things on earth or things in heaven, by making peace through his blood, shed on the cross.

COLOSSIANS 1:19–20

Let us not love with words or speech but with actions and in truth. This is how we know that we belong to the truth and how we set our hearts at rest in his presence: If our hearts condemn us, we know that God is greater than our hearts, and he knows everything.

1 JOHN 3:18–20

"Two people owed money to a certain moneylender. One owed him five hundred denarii, and the other fifty. Neither of them had the money to pay him back, so he forgave the debts of both. Now which of them will love him more?"

Simon replied, "I suppose the one who had the bigger debt forgiven."

"You have judged correctly," Jesus said.

LUKE 7:41–43

*Devotional Thought on*
# FORGIVENESS

The word *hate* was rarely used around our house. Very early in their lives, our daughters learned that, unless they were talking about monsters or poisonous snakes, they couldn't use this term.

Notwithstanding this house rule that I personally enforced, there was an object I grew up hating as much as monsters and poisonous snakes. The object was a black-and-gray-speckled, spiral-bound, eight-by-ten book, and each of my teachers had one on his or her desk. Printed on the cover were the words "Student Records."

Why did I feel so strongly? Because these record books contained inside information about me. They recorded every late paper, every failing grade, every citizenship faux pas . . . everything I didn't want anyone to know.

King David lived a life filled with tardiness, failure, and poor citizenship. And he knew what it was to have all of these marks indelibly inscribed on the public record.

Because of his willingness to confess his sin, is it any wonder that David wrote the opening lines to Psalm 32: "Blessed is the one whose transgressions are forgiven, whose sins are covered"(v. 1)? Can you blame him for referring to the forgiven person as "blessed"? It's as though the despised record book found its way to the desk's precipice, fell into the trash can, and was delivered to the city dump for burning.

Confess your sins. Watch them burn. Then bask in the love and embrace of your Teacher and Savior.

# God's Words of Life on
# FRIENDSHIP

One who has unreliable friends soon comes to ruin,

but there is a friend who sticks closer than a

brother.

PROVERBS 18:24

Two are better than one,

because they have a good return for their labor:

If either of them falls down,

one can help the other up.

But pity anyone who falls

and has no one to help them up.

Also, if two lie down together, they will keep warm.

But how can one keep warm alone?

Though one may be overpowered,

two can defend themselves.

A cord of three strands is not quickly broken.

ECCLESIASTES 4:9–12

Wounds from a friend can be trusted.

PROVERBS 27:6

Perfume and incense bring joy to the heart,
　　and the pleasantness of a friend
　　springs from their heartfelt advice.

PROVERBS 27:9

Be devoted to one another in love. Honor one another above yourselves.

ROMANS 12:10

If we walk in the light, as [God] is in the light, we have fellowship with one another.

1 JOHN 1:7

"Greater love has no one than this: to lay down one's life for one's friends. You are my friends if you do what I command. I no longer call you servants, because a servant does not know his master's business. Instead, I have called you friends."

JOHN 15:13–15

A friend loves at all times,
　　and a brother is born for a time of adversity.

PROVERBS 17:17

My intercessor is my friend
　　as my eyes pour out tears to God.

JOB 16:20

One who loves a pure heart and who speaks with grace
will have the king for a friend.

PROVERBS 22:11

Ruth replied [to Naomi], . . . "Where you go I will go, and where you stay I will stay. Your people will be my people and your God my God. Where you die I will die, and there I will be buried. May the LORD deal with me, be it ever so severely, if even death separates you and me."

RUTH 1:16–17

*Devotional Thought on*
# FRIENDSHIP

Jesus tells us to love everyone, even our enemies (Luke 6:27, 35). But Proverbs 13:20 says that if we are to grow wise, we must walk with wise people. If we choose "fools" as companions, we'll suffer harm.

A "companion" is much more than an acquaintance; he or she is one who becomes a close friend, a traveling buddy, even a mate. If we choose companions who don't love God or don't act according to His Word, we're told in no uncertain terms that we're walking straight into trouble.

As dads, we know our job is to protect our children from harm. Therefore our job is to teach them to choose friends wisely. And this lesson is every bit as important for us as it is for our kids. Our companions are either making us wiser or leading us right into harm's way.

The Bible doesn't contradict itself at all on this issue. Love your neighbor. Love your enemy. But choose your friends with care.

# God's Words of Life on
## GIVING

He who supplies seed to the sower and bread for food will also supply and increase your store of seed and will enlarge the harvest of your righteousness. You will be enriched in every way so that you can be generous on every occasion, and through us your generosity will result in thanksgiving to God.

This service that you perform is not only supplying the needs of the Lord's people but is also overflowing in many expressions of thanks to God. Because of the service by which you have proved yourselves, others will praise God for the obedience that accompanies your confession of the gospel of Christ, and for your generosity in sharing with them and with everyone else.

2 Corinthians 9:10–13

If they obey and serve [God],
   they will spend the rest of their days in prosperity
   and their years in contentment.

Job 36:11

Jesus sat down opposite the place where the offerings were put and watched the crowd putting their money into the temple treasury. Many rich people threw in large amounts. But a poor widow came and put in two very small copper coins, worth only a few cents.

Calling his disciples to him, Jesus said, "Truly I tell you, this poor widow has put more into the treasury than all the others. They all gave out of their wealth; but she, out of her poverty, put in everything—all she had to live on."

MARK 12:41–44

"Bring the whole tithe into the storehouse, that there may be food in my house. Test me in this," says the LORD Almighty, "and see if I will not throw open the floodgates of heaven and pour out so much blessing that there will not be room enough to store it."

MALACHI 3:10

Be openhanded and freely lend [the poor] whatever they need. . . . Give generously to them and do so without a grudging heart; then because of this the LORD your God will bless you in all your work and in everything you put your hand to.

DEUTERONOMY 15:8, 10

"Give, and it will be given to you. A good measure, pressed down, shaken together and running over, will be poured into your lap. For with the measure you use, it will be measured to you."

LUKE 6:38

"Store up for yourselves treasures in heaven, where moths and vermin do not destroy, and where thieves do not break in and steal. For where your treasure is, there your heart will be also."

MATTHEW 6:20–21

"It is more blessed to give than to receive."

ACTS 20:35

Do not forget to do good and to share with others, for with such sacrifices God is pleased.

HEBREWS 13:16

Whoever sows sparingly will also reap sparingly, and whoever sows generously will also reap generously. Each of you should give what you have decided in your heart to give, not reluctantly or under compulsion, for God loves a cheerful giver. And God is able to bless you abundantly, so that in all things at all times, having all that you need, you will abound in every good work.

2 CORINTHIANS 9:6–8

God is not unjust; he will not forget your work and the love you have shown him as you have helped his people and continue to help them.

HEBREWS 6:10

"If anyone gives even a cup of cold water to one of these little ones who is my disciple, truly I tell you, that person will certainly not lose their reward."

MATTHEW 10:42

The generous will themselves be blessed,
> for they share their food with the poor.

PROVERBS 22:9

Whoever refreshes others will be refreshed.

PROVERBS 11:25

Whoever is kind to the poor lends to the LORD,
> and he will reward them for what they have done.

PROVERBS 19:17

Honor the LORD with your wealth,
> with the firstfruits of all your crops;
then your barns will be filled to overflowing,
> and your vats will brim over with new wine.

PROVERBS 3:9–10

If you spend yourselves in behalf of the hungry
　　and satisfy the needs of the oppressed,
then your light will rise in the darkness,
　　and your night will become like the noonday.
The Lord will guide you always;
　　he will satisfy your needs in a sun-scorched land
　　and will strengthen your frame.
You will be like a well-watered garden,
　　like a spring whose waters never fail.

Isaiah 58:10–11

"The King will say, . . . 'I was hungry and you gave me something to eat, I was thirsty and you gave me something to drink, I was a stranger and you invited me in, I needed clothes and you clothed me, I was sick and you looked after me, I was in prison and you came to visit me.'

"Then the righteous will answer him, 'Lord, when did we see you hungry and feed you, or thirsty and give you something to drink? When did we see you a stranger and invite you in, or needing clothes and clothe you? When did we see you sick or in prison and go to visit you?'

"The King will reply, 'Truly I tell you, whatever you did for one of the least of these brothers and sisters of mine, you did for me.'"

Matthew 25:34–40

## *Devotional Thought on*
# GIVING

As incredible as this sounds, my grandfather never locked the doors of his home. "If someone comes to our house in need, they're welcome to anything we have here," he told me. As a child, I never saw my dad handle an offering plate without putting something into it—even on vacation. No doubt he also wanted his children to witness the satisfaction of giving.

Because I had seen this modeled and truly didn't know any other way to act, our girls will tell you that, thanks to his dad and his grandfather, their dad does the same thing. There is joy in the simple act of giving. Stewardship is its own reward. Another way of saying this might be that a man is measured not by how much he has but by how much he gives away.

The members of the early church knew about this. They "shared everything they had. . . . There were no needy persons among them" (Acts 4:32, 34). Those who had been blessed with possessions turned their attention away from their own success and lavished their good fortune on others.

Dads can be the best teachers on the subject of giving. How generous will your children be?

# God's Words of Life on
# GOD'S CARE

"I am the good shepherd. The good shepherd
lays down his life for the sheep."

JOHN 10:11

The righteous cry out, and the LORD hears them;
    he delivers them from all their troubles.
The LORD is close to the brokenhearted
    and saves those who are crushed in spirit.

PSALM 34:17–18

"Look at the birds of the air; they do not sow or reap or
store away in barns, and yet your heavenly Father feeds
them. Are you not much more valuable than they?"

MATTHEW 6:26

"Do not be afraid, little flock, for your Father has been
pleased to give you the kingdom."

LUKE 12:32

LORD, you establish peace for us;
    all that we have accomplished you have done for us.

ISAIAH 26:12

"My sheep listen to my voice; I know them, and they follow me. I give them eternal life, and they shall never perish; no one will snatch them out of my hand. My Father, who has given them to me, is greater than all; no one can snatch them out of my Father's hand."

JOHN 10:27–29

Praise the LORD, my soul,
>      and forget not all his benefits—
who forgives all your sins
>      and heals all your diseases,
who redeems your life from the pit
>      and crowns you with love and compassion,
who satisfies your desires with good things
>      so that your youth is renewed like the eagle's.

PSALM 103:2–5

The eyes of all look to you,
>      and you give them their food at the proper time.
You open your hand
>      and satisfy the desires of every living thing.

PSALM 145:15–16

Praise be to the Lord, to God our Savior,
>      who daily bears our burdens.

PSALM 68:19

You, Lord, have helped me and comforted me.

PSALM 86:17

The Lord will keep you from all harm—
he will watch over your life;
the Lord will watch over your coming and going
both now and forevermore.

PSALM 121:7–8

"Surely I am with you always, to the very end of the age."

MATTHEW 28:20

"The Lord your God is with you,
the Mighty Warrior who saves.
He will take great delight in you;
in his love he will no longer rebuke you,
but will rejoice over you with singing."

ZEPHANIAH 3:17

[The Lord] tends his flock like a shepherd:
He gathers the lambs in his arms
and carries them close to his heart;
he gently leads those that have young.

ISAIAH 40:11

*Devotional Thought on*
# GOD'S CARE

One summer we were castle-hopping in Europe. These structures were unbelievable. As I was standing in the courtyard of one particular palace and studying the intricate stonework, something dawned on me. These structures weren't just fancy homes; they were fortresses, built to protect a king's or nobleman's family and a few hundred of his closest friends during hostile times. The thick walls, towering turrets, and drawbridges were more than mere decoration.

You and I live in a war zone. The internal and external forces that seek to take us and our families hostage are as real today as the warriors who once tried to besiege those European castles. But God has built up our homes to be like fortresses; He protects them with His own foot soldiers.

When we overlook the fact that we are living in a war zone, our appreciation for God's loving protection diminishes in value. But when we truly pay attention to this fact, our hearts should be filled with gratitude for His wings, His eyes, His hands, and His tireless angels standing guard.

# *God's Words of Life on*
# HOPE

This God is our God for ever and ever;
>    he will be our guide even to the end.

PSALM 48:14

You discern my going out and my lying down;
>    you are familiar with all my ways.

PSALM 139:3

You are God my Savior,
and my hope is in you all day long.

PSALM 25:5

Put your hope in the LORD,
>    for with the LORD is unfailing love
>    and with him is full redemption.

PSALM 130:7

We have put our hope in the living God, who is the
Savior of all people, and especially of those who believe.

1 TIMOTHY 4:10

Put your hope in the LORD
>> both now and forevermore.

PSALM 131:3

Devote your heart to [God]
>> and stretch out your hands to him. . . .
You will be secure, because there is hope;
>> you will look about you and take your rest in safety.

JOB 11:13, 18

Yes, my soul, find rest in God;
>> my hope comes from him.

PSALM 62:5

Wisdom is like honey for you:
>> If you find it, there is a future hope for you,
>> and your hope will not be cut off.

PROVERBS 24:14

"You will know that I am the LORD;
>> those who hope in me will not be disappointed."

ISAIAH 49:23

Against all hope, Abraham in hope believed and so
became the father of many nations.

ROMANS 4:18

Hope does not put us to shame, because God's love has been poured out into our hearts through the Holy Spirit, who has been given to us.

ROMANS 5:5

You believe in God, who raised [Christ] from the dead and glorified him, and so your faith and hope are in God.

1 PETER 1:21

*Devotional Thought on*
# HOPE

Only twice in my life have I tried my hand at organized football, but in my limited involvement, I have had the experience of knowing what "the pile" feels like. This happens when the ball carrier is tackled and those closest to him, whether teammates or opponents, pile themselves up like cordwood on this hapless player. One consistent football rule from junior high to the big time is: when the play is over, no additional players can join the pile. In other words, no piling on.

As you read the book of Job, you realize that every single person who knew Job had piled on top of him. At times he even thought he felt God's heft on the pile. But Job 19:25, "I know that my redeemer lives," was uttered in the crush of this setting.

Some days we can truly identify with Job under the pile. The verse's encouragement is a simple one, though. Regardless of the weight, the pain, the frustration, the inability to breathe under the pressure, our God is still standing. Take a deep breath. Look up from the mash and be glad. Your Redeemer has come.

# God's Words of Life on
# IDENTITY

God said, "Let us make mankind in our image,
in our likeness, so that they may rule over the
fish in the sea and the birds in the sky, over the
livestock and all the wild animals, and over all
the creatures that move along the ground."

So God created mankind in his own image,
in the image of God he created them;
male and female he created them.

GENESIS 1:26–27

You created my inmost being;
you knit me together in my mother's womb.
I praise you because I am fearfully and wonderfully made;
your works are wonderful,
I know that full well.

PSALM 139:13–14

"Before I formed you in the womb I knew you,
before you were born I set you apart."

JEREMIAH 1:5

Do you not know that your bodies are temples of the Holy Spirit, who is in you, whom you have received from God? You are not your own; you were bought at a price. Therefore honor God with your bodies.

1 CORINTHIANS 6:19–20

*Devotional Thought on*

# IDENTITY

There is one area of my life—and yours—in which there is no need for competition. This truth comes through clearly in the words of Jeremiah's call: "Before you were born I set you apart" (Jeremiah 1:5). In other words, God was saying to this prophet, "You're one of a kind, Jeremiah. I have no templates, no stencils. You can look around all you want, but you're the only man who is just like you."

Please do not miss this spellbinding truth: there is no competition in God's plan for you and me. His calling is as individualized as each person's fingerprint; it belongs to no one else.

Does this mean that before my parents had ever met, God had a specific work for me to accomplish? Yes, it does. And does this mean that if I want to discover the greatest joy in living, I need to take my focus away from others and tenaciously seek God's singular direction for me? Again, the answer is in the affirmative.

What has God called you to? Whatever it is, it's all yours. There's no winning or losing in this game . . . there's only obedience.

# God's Words of Life on
# INTEGRITY

In everything set . . . an example by doing what is good. In your teaching show integrity, seriousness and soundness of speech that cannot be condemned.

TITUS 2:7–8

The LORD . . . delights in people who are trustworthy.

PROVERBS 12:22

Blessed is the one who does not condemn himself by what he approves.

ROMANS 14:22

To do what is right and just
    is more acceptable to the LORD than sacrifice.

PROVERBS 21:3

I put in charge of Jerusalem my brother Hanani, along with Hananiah the commander of the citadel, because he was a man of integrity and feared God more than most people do.

NEHEMIAH 7:2

Honest scales and balances belong to the LORD;
> all the weights in the bag are of his making.

PROVERBS 16:11

We are taking pains to do what is right, not only in the eyes of the Lord but also in the eyes of man.

2 CORINTHIANS 8:21

Obey your earthly masters in everything; and do it, not only when their eye is on you and to curry their favor, but with sincerity of heart and reverence for the Lord. Whatever you do, work at it with all your heart, as working for the Lord, not for human masters, since you know that you will receive an inheritance from the Lord as a reward. It is the Lord Christ you are serving.

COLOSSIANS 3:22–24

The integrity of the upright guides them,
> but the unfaithful are destroyed by their duplicity.

PROVERBS 11:3

Make it your ambition to lead a quiet life: You should mind your own business and work with your hands, . . . so that your daily life may win the respect of outsiders and so that you will not be dependent on anybody.

1 THESSALONIANS 4:11–12

Live such good lives among [unbelievers] that, though they accuse you of doing wrong, they may see your good deeds and glorify God on the day he visits us.

1 PETER 2:12

Let the LORD judge the peoples.
Vindicate me, LORD, according to my righteousness,
　　according to my integrity, O Most High.

PSALM 7:8

Whoever walks in integrity walks securely,
　　but whoever takes crooked paths will be found out.

PROVERBS 10:9

He has shown you, O mortal, what is good.
　　And what does the LORD require of you?
To act justly and to love mercy
　　and to walk humbly with your God.

MICAH 6:8

I know, my God, that you test the heart and are pleased with integrity.

1 CHRONICLES 29:17

Righteousness guards the person of integrity.

PROVERBS 13:6

The LORD . . . takes the upright into his confidence.

PROVERBS 3:32

May integrity and uprightness protect me,
  because my hope, LORD, is in you. . . .
Vindicate me, LORD,
  for I have led a blameless life;
I have trusted in the LORD
  and have not faltered.
Test me, LORD, and try me,
  examine my heart and my mind;
for I have always been mindful of your unfailing love
  and have lived in reliance on your faithfulness.

PSALM 25:21; 26:1–3

I strive always to keep my conscience clear before God
and man.

ACTS 24:16

Whatever is true, whatever is noble, whatever is
right, whatever is pure, whatever is lovely, whatever is
admirable—if anything is excellent or praiseworthy—
think about such things.

PHILIPPIANS 4:8

Stand firm . . . with the belt of truth buckled around
your waist, with the breastplate of righteousness in
place, and with your feet fitted with the readiness that
comes from the gospel of peace.

EPHESIANS 6:14–15

*Devotional Thought on*
# INTEGRITY

The apostle Paul declared, "I strive always to keep my conscience clear before God and man" (Acts 24:16). Imagine the courage, confidence, and self-assurance it took to say such a thing in the face of one's accusers.

What does it mean to have a clear conscience? It means that you can say with a straight face, "I have done everything I can do. There are no sins to confess. Look wherever you want, but there will be no surprises."

We are living in a time when men are quietly scrambling to hide from their pasts. Every day we hear of yet another man whose treacherous history is brought into the light of day.

Where are the Pauls? Where are the men who live with clear consciences? Do we live our lives just one small step ahead of the truth of our pasts, or do we rest because we've withheld no secrets?

You may have some confessions to submit, a record to clear up. There could be consequences. But my guess is that Paul would promise us that a soul vindicated from full disclosure is well worth any price we may have to pay. Regardless of the cost, it'll be worth it.

# God's Words of Life on
## JOY

Light shines on the righteous
  and joy on the upright in heart.

PSALM 97:11

He will yet fill your mouth with laughter
  and your lips with shouts of joy.

JOB 8:21

His favor lasts a lifetime;
weeping may stay for the night,
  but rejoicing comes in the morning.

PSALM 30:5

Rejoice in the LORD and be glad, you righteous;
  sing, all you who are upright in heart!

PSALM 32:11

The righteous will rejoice in the LORD
  and take refuge in him;
  all the upright in heart will glory in him!

PSALM 64:10

Shout for joy to the LORD, all the earth.

Worship the LORD with gladness;

come before him with joyful songs.

PSALM 100:1–2

"As the Father has loved me, so have I loved you. Now remain in my love. If you keep my commands, you will remain in my love, just as I have kept my Father's commands and remain in his love. I have told you this so that my joy may be in you and that your joy may be complete."

JOHN 15:9–11

May all who seek you

rejoice and be glad in you;

may those who long for your saving help always say,

"The LORD is great!"

PSALM 70:4

Those the LORD has rescued will return.

They will enter Zion with singing;

everlasting joy will crown their heads.

Gladness and joy will overtake them,

and sorrow and sighing will flee away.

ISAIAH 51:11

Let all who take refuge in you be glad;
>> let them ever sing for joy.
Spread your protection over them,
>> that those who love your name may rejoice in you.

PSALM 5:11

I rejoice in following your statutes
>> as one rejoices in great riches.

PSALM 119:14

Those who sow with tears
>> will reap with songs of joy.

PSALM 126:5

The prospect of the righteous is joy.

PROVERBS 10:28

You will go out in joy
>> and be led forth in peace;
the mountains and hills
>> will burst into song before you,
and all the trees of the field
>> will clap their hands.

ISAIAH 55:12

Rejoice in the Lord your God,

> for he has given you the autumn rains
>
> because he is faithful.

He sends you abundant showers,

> both autumn and spring rains, as before.

Joel 2:23

"Until now you have not asked for anything in my name.
Ask and you will receive, and your joy will be complete."

John 16:24

You have made known to me the paths of life;

> you will fill me with joy in your presence.

Acts 2:28

The kingdom of God is . . . righteousness, peace and joy
in the Holy Spirit.

Romans 14:17

Rejoice in the Lord always. I will say it again: Rejoice!

Philippians 4:4

Rejoice always.

1 Thessalonians 5:16

May the God of hope fill you with all joy and peace as you trust in him, so that you may overflow with hope by the power of the Holy Spirit.

ROMANS 15:13

The joy of the LORD is your strength.

NEHEMIAH 8:10

The LORD has done great things for us,
and we are filled with joy.

PSALM 126:3

"Blessed are you when people hate you,
when they exclude you and insult you
and reject your name as evil,
because of the Son of Man.
"Rejoice in that day and leap for joy, because
great is your reward in heaven."

LUKE 6:22–23

The precepts of the LORD are right,
giving joy to the heart.
The commands of the LORD are radiant,
giving light to the eyes.

PSALM 19:8

Your statutes are my heritage forever;

> they are the joy of my heart.

We wait in hope for the LORD;

> he is our help and our shield.

In him our hearts rejoice,

> for we trust in his holy name.

PSALM 33:20–21

I delight greatly in the LORD;

> my soul rejoices in my God.

For he has clothed me with garments of salvation.

ISAIAH 61:10

My heart rejoices in the LORD;

> in the LORD my horn is lifted high.

1 SAMUEL 2:1

My soul glorifies the Lord

> and my spirit rejoices in God my Savior.

LUKE 1:46–47

You believe in [Jesus Christ] and are filled with an inexpressible and glorious joy.

1 PETER 1:8

Let us rejoice and be glad
    and give him glory!
For the wedding of the Lamb has come,
    and his bride has made herself ready.

REVELATION 19:7

I will rejoice in the LORD,
    I will be joyful in God my Savior.
The Sovereign LORD is my strength;
        he makes my feet like the feet of a deer,
        he enables me to tread on the heights.

HABAKKUK 3:18–19

One generation commends your works to another;
    they tell of your mighty acts.
They speak of the glorious splendor of your majesty—
    and I will meditate on your wonderful works.
They tell of the power of your awesome works—
    and I will proclaim your great deeds.
They celebrate your abundant goodness
    and joyfully sing of your righteousness.

PSALM 145:4–7

*Devotional Thought on*

# JOY

The story of the Philippian jailer is one of the Bible's most remarkable stories of how God's grace can affect a father. Here was a man faced with the trauma of failure on the job. Jailers not only got fired when prisoners escaped; they often lost their lives. Following a midnight earthquake that turned the prison to rubble, the jailer was preparing to take his life. Paul and Silas shouted at the jailer, who was about to impale himself on his sword, "We are all here!" (Acts 16:28). Completely overwhelmed by this act of mercy, the jailer fell to his knees before his gracious captives. "Sirs," he cried, "what must I do to be saved?" (Acts 16:30).

That night, not only was the jailer brought into a relationship with God, but he also invited Paul and Silas to his home. As a result, the jailer "was filled with joy because he had come to believe in God—he and his whole household" (Acts 16:34).

Confess your sinfulness, enjoy His grace, then let your experience with Christ infect your family. Let it bring joy to your home.

# God's Words of Life on
# KINDNESS

Good will come to those who are generous and lend freely,
who conduct their affairs with justice.

PSALM 112:5

Blessed is the one who is kind to the needy.

PROVERBS 14:21

"Give to the one who asks you, and do not turn away
from the one who wants to borrow from you."

MATTHEW 5:42

"Come, you who are blessed by my Father; take your
inheritance, the kingdom prepared for you since the
creation of the world. For I was hungry and you gave
me something to eat, I was thirsty and you gave me
something to drink, I was a stranger and you invited me
in, I needed clothes and you clothed me, I was sick and
you looked after me, I was in prison and you came to
visit me."

MATTHEW 25:34–36

Love is kind.

1 Corinthians 13:4

Carry each other's burdens, and in this way you will fulfill the law of Christ.

Galatians 6:2

As we have opportunity, let us do good to all people.

Galatians 6:10

As God's chosen people, holy and dearly loved, clothe yourselves with compassion, kindness, humility, gentleness and patience.

Colossians 3:12

Make every effort to add to your faith . . . mutual affection; and to mutual affection, love. For if you possess these qualities in increasing measure, they will keep you from being ineffective and unproductive in your knowledge of our Lord Jesus Christ.

2 Peter 1:5, 7–8

If anyone has material possessions and sees a brother or sister in need but has no pity on them, how can the love of God be in that person? Dear children, let us not love with words or speech but with actions and in truth.

1 John 3:17–18

[Ruth] bowed down with her face to the ground. She asked him, "Why have I found such favor in your eyes that you notice me—a foreigner?"

Boaz replied, "I've been told all about what you have done for your mother-in-law since the death of your husband—how you left your father and mother and your homeland and came to live with a people you did not know before. May the LORD repay you for what you have done. May you be richly rewarded by the LORD, the God of Israel, under whose wings you have come to take refuge."

RUTH 2:10–12

The fruit of the Spirit is love, joy, peace, forbearance, kindness, goodness, faithfulness, gentleness and self-control.

GALATIANS 5:22–23

When the kindness and love of God our Savior appeared, he saved us, not because of righteous things we had done, but because of his mercy.

TITUS 3:4–5

"If anyone gives even a cup of cold water to one of these little ones who is my disciple, truly I tell you, that person will certainly not lose their reward."

MATTHEW 10:42

# KINDNESS

Have you ever tried to sympathize with a child who's suffered a scuffed knee without squatting down and stooping to his or her level? Of course such a thing is impossible. Unless a child sees the understanding on your face and sees it down on his or her level, that child won't be able to accept your comfort.

The psalmist David saw that God demonstrated this kind of care for His children. David called it "compassion": "Praise the LORD, . . . who forgives all your sins and heals all your diseases" (Psalm 103:2–3). God the Father takes moments from His busy schedule—keeping the stars and planets on their charted courses, growing food for a hungry world, raising up and bringing down world leaders—to stoop to our level and have compassion on His bumped and bruised children.

You're a busy man. You've got places to go, people to see, deals to get done. But our busy heavenly Father, the Creator of the universe, has compassion. He's never too busy to stop, never too proud to stoop. It's a good thing too. How else could we ever see His face?

Look carefully—this Father's got lots of love. He stops, then He stoops. I guess if He can do it, so can we.

# God's Words of Life on
## LOVE

"Love each other as I have loved you."

John 15:12

Be devoted to one another in love. Honor one another above yourselves.

Romans 12:10

Serve one another humbly in love.

Galatians 5:13

You yourselves have been taught by God to love each other.

1 Thessalonians 4:9

How good and pleasant it is
when God's people live together in unity!

Psalm 133:1

Walk in the way of love, just as Christ loved us and gave himself up for us as a fragrant offering and sacrifice to God.

Ephesians 5:2

May the Lord make your love increase and overflow for each other and for everyone else.

1 Thessalonians 3:12

Keep on loving one another.

Hebrews 13:1

Be like-minded, be sympathetic, love one another, be compassionate and humble.

1 Peter 3:8

Love does no harm to a neighbor. Therefore love is the fulfillment of the law.

Romans 13:10

Love . . . comes from a pure heart and a good conscience and a sincere faith.

1 Timothy 1:5

As God's chosen people, holy and dearly loved, clothe yourselves with compassion, kindness, humility, gentleness and patience. . . . Over all these virtues put on love, which binds them all together in perfect unity.

Colossians 3:12, 14

Do everything in love.

1 Corinthians 16:14

Many waters cannot quench love;

    rivers cannot sweep it away.

If one were to give

    all the wealth of one's house for love,

    it would be utterly scorned.

Song of Songs 8:7

"You have heard that it was said, 'Love your neighbor and hate your enemy.' But I tell you, love your enemies and pray for those who persecute you."

Matthew 5:43–44

Let no debt remain outstanding, except the continuing debt to love one another, for whoever loves others has fulfilled the law.

Romans 13:8

This is love: that we walk in obedience to [God's] commands. As you have heard from the beginning, his command is that you walk in love.

2 John v. 6

See what great love the Father has lavished on us, that we should be called children of God! And that is what we are!

1 John 3:1

Praise be to the LORD,

for he showed me the wonders of his love.

PSALM 31:21

How priceless is your unfailing love, O God!

People take refuge in the shadow of your wings.

PSALM 36:7

I will sing of the LORD's great love forever;

with my mouth I will make your faithfulness known

through all generations.

PSALM 89:1

God demonstrates his own love for us in this: While we were still sinners, Christ died for us.

ROMANS 5:8

I pray that you, being rooted and established in love, may have power . . . to grasp how wide and long and high and deep is the love of Christ.

EPHESIANS 3:17–18

Let us love one another, for love comes from God. Everyone who loves has been born of God and knows God. Whoever does not love does not know God, because God is love.

1 JOHN 4:7–8

If I speak in the tongues of men or of angels, but do not have love, I am only a resounding gong or a clanging cymbal. If I have the gift of prophecy and can fathom all mysteries and all knowledge, and if I have a faith that can move mountains, but do not have love, I am nothing. If I give all I possess to the poor and give over my body to hardship that I may boast, but do not have love, I gain nothing.

Love is patient, love is kind. It does not envy, it does not boast, it is not proud. It does not dishonor others, it is not self-seeking, it is not easily angered, it keeps no record of wrongs. Love does not delight in evil but rejoices with the truth. It always protects, always trusts, always hopes, always perseveres.

Love never fails.

1 CORINTHIANS 13:1–8

The only thing that counts is faith expressing itself through love.

GALATIANS 5:6

Because of his great love for us, God, who is rich in mercy, made us alive with Christ even when we were dead in transgressions.

EPHESIANS 2:4–5

This is love: not that we loved God, but that he loved us and sent his Son as an atoning sacrifice for our sins.

1 John 4:10

Now that you have purified yourselves by obeying the truth so that you have sincere love for each other, love one another deeply, from the heart.

1 Peter 1:22

No one has ever seen God; but if we love one another, God lives in us and his love is made complete in us.

1 John 4:12

God so loved the world that he gave his one and only Son, that whoever believes in him shall not perish but have eternal life.

John 3:16

This is how we know what love is: Jesus Christ laid down his life for us. And we ought to lay down our lives for our brothers and sisters.

1 John 3:16

Love each other deeply, because love covers over a multitude of sins.

1 Peter 4:8

*Devotional Thought on*

# LOVE

We will hear the word *love* spoken today. We may even speak it ourselves. But lest we consign this word to a child's penny valentine or a whimpering teenager expressing himself in a love note, we cannot forget its unmistakable power.

The phrase "I love you" changed your life. Once you were a single man, free to move about at will; "I love you" inextricably bound you to one woman for the rest of your life. "I love you" gave you a child—a little person who relentlessly watches your every move, keeping you on the straight and narrow.

"I love you" opened our heavenly Father's hand to welcome us, sinful as we were, to Himself. "I love you" gave us Jesus, who endured the cross for those sins.

"I love you" is about the serious stuff of life. Its impact changes people. Its power moves them away from their complacency. It alters their plans. It renders them speechless.

You love your family. Your family loves you. Love changes everything.

# God's Words of Life on
# MARRIAGE

Husbands ought to love their wives as their own bodies. He who loves his wife loves himself. After all, no one ever hated their own body, but they feed and care for their body, just as Christ does the church—for we are members of his body. "For this reason a man will leave his father and mother and be united to his wife, and the two will become one flesh."

EPHESIANS 5:28–31

You are altogether beautiful, my darling;
    there is no flaw in you. . . .
You have stolen my heart, my sister, my bride;
    you have stolen my heart
with one glance of your eyes,
    with one jewel of your necklace.
How delightful is your love, my sister, my bride!
    How much more pleasing is your love than wine,
and the fragrance of your perfume
    more than any spice!

SONG OF SONGS 4:7, 9–10

Place me like a seal over your heart,
    like a seal on your arm;
for love is as strong as death,
    its jealousy unyielding as the grave.
It burns like blazing fire,
    like a mighty flame.
Many waters cannot quench love;
    rivers cannot sweep it away.
If one were to give
    all the wealth of one's house for love,
    it would be utterly scorned.

SONG OF SONGS 8:6–7

A wife of noble character who can find?
    She is worth far more than rubies.
Her husband has full confidence in her
    and lacks nothing of value.
She brings him good, not harm,
    all the days of her life. . . .
Her children arise and call her blessed;
    her husband also, and he praises her:
"Many women do noble things,
    but you surpass them all."

PROVERBS 31:10–12, 28–29

Enjoy life with your wife, whom you love.

ECCLESIASTES 9:9

Arise, my darling,
my beautiful one, come with me.
See! The winter is past;
the rains are over and gone.
Flowers appear on the earth;
the season of singing has come,
the cooing of doves
is heard in our land.

SONG OF SONGS 2:10–12

## Devotional Thought on
# MARRIAGE

Do you remember your first love? Do you remember how you "accidentally" let your hand brush against hers, hoping she would not resist? Do you remember collecting the courage to kiss a girl for the first time? And how about the excitement of pursuing the woman who would one day become your wife?

Although the tender words of love you used to speak have been eclipsed by discussions about schedules, car pools, and trash in the kitchen, your wife still needs the romance of your first embrace.

Do something today that takes you back to those days of high school love. Be daring. Lavish her with something she doesn't expect. You never know when the bell will ring and this golden opportunity will end. Recess never lasts long enough.

# God's Words of Life on
## MONEY

Whoever gathers money little by little makes it grow.

PROVERBS 13:11

Wisdom is a shelter
    as money is a shelter,
but the advantage of knowledge is this:
    Wisdom preserves those who have it.

ECCLESIASTES 7:12

Command those who are rich in this present world not
to be arrogant nor to put their hope in wealth, which
is so uncertain, but to put their hope in God, who
richly provides us with everything for our enjoyment.
Command them to do good, to be rich in good deeds,
and to be generous and willing to share. In this way they
will lay up treasure for themselves as a firm foundation
for the coming age, so that they may take hold of the life
that is truly life.

1 TIMOTHY 6:17–19

"No one can serve two masters. Either you will hate the one and love the other, or you will be devoted to the one and despise the other. You cannot serve both God and money."

MATTHEW 6:24

"Do not store up for yourselves treasures on earth, where moths and vermin destroy, and where thieves break in and steal. But store up for yourselves treasures in heaven, where moths and vermin do not destroy, and where thieves do not break in and steal."

MATTHEW 6:19–20

Keep your lives free from the love of money and be content with what you have.

HEBREWS 13:5

Remember the LORD your God, for it is he who gives you the ability to produce wealth, and so confirms his covenant, which he swore to your ancestors, as it is today.

DEUTERONOMY 8:18

God will meet all your needs according to the riches of his glory in Christ Jesus.

PHILIPPIANS 4:19

"Whoever can be trusted with very little can also be trusted with much."

LUKE 16:10

Turn my heart toward your statutes
    and not toward selfish gain.

PSALM 119:36

"Use worldly wealth to gain friends for yourselves, so that when it is gone, you will be welcomed into eternal dwellings."

LUKE 16:9

Why spend money on what is not bread,
    and your labor on what does not satisfy?
Listen, listen to me, and eat what is good,
    and you will delight in the richest of fare.

ISAIAH 55:2

## Devotional Thought on
# MONEY

*T*ithing is a word that means giving 10 percent of our income to further God's work in the world. By tithing, we show God that we are thankful for the blessings He's given us. When we tithe, we also acknowledge that God owns everything we have anyway and that we want to honor Him by giving some of that back to Him.

Tithing is a part of God's plan to keep His church in order. Our tithes go to pay the staff's salaries, cover the bills for the church, and help others who are needy. It's important to God that we honor Him with our finances. Through the prophet Malachi, the Lord told the Israelites to tithe faithfully. "Test me in this," He said, "and see if I will not throw open the floodgates of heaven and pour out so much blessing that there will not be room enough to store it" (Malachi 3:10).

And one more thing: we don't honor God so that He will honor us; we honor Him because He's God, and He deserves it. Look at how He's already blessed you, then consider how much of what you own comes from God's hand.

# God's Words of Life on
# OBEDIENCE

This is how we know that we love the children of
God: by loving God and carrying out his commands.
In fact, this is love for God: to keep his commands.
And his commands are not burdensome.

1 John 5:2–3

"If you walk in obedience to me and keep my decrees
and commands . . . , I will give you a long life."

1 Kings 3:14

I have considered my ways
    and have turned my steps to your statutes.
I will hasten and not delay
    to obey your commands.

Psalm 119:59–60

The one who keeps God's commands lives in him, and
he in them. And this is how we know that he lives in us:
We know it by the Spirit he gave us.

1 John 3:24

We will serve the LORD our God and obey him.

JOSHUA 24:24

All the ways of the LORD are loving and faithful
toward those who keep the demands of his
covenant.

PSALM 25:10

I have kept my feet from every evil path
so that I might obey your word.

PSALM 119:101

From everlasting to everlasting
the LORD's love is with those who fear him,
and his righteousness with their children's
children—
with those who keep his covenant
and remember to obey his precepts.

PSALM 103:17–18

Blessed are those who keep his statutes
and seek him with all their heart—
they do no wrong
but follow his ways.

PSALM 119:2–3

If anyone obeys his word, love for God is truly made complete in them.

1 John 2:5

Whoever keeps commandments keeps their life.

Proverbs 19:16

"Obey me, and I will be your God and you will be my people. Walk in obedience to all I command you, that it may go well with you."

Jeremiah 7:23

"Anyone who loves me will obey my teaching. My Father will love them, and we will come to them and make our home with them."

John 14:23

Have confidence in your leaders and submit to their authority, because they keep watch over you as those who must give an account. Do this so that their work will be a joy, not a burden.

Hebrews 13:17

To love [God] with all your heart, with all your understanding and with all your strength, and to love your neighbor as yourself is more important than all burnt offerings and sacrifices.

Mark 12:33

*Devotional Thought on*
# OBEDIENCE

God stepped up with what seemed like a cruel assignment. "Kill your boy," God told an astonished Abraham. "Sacrifice him to Me" (Genesis 22). What an incomprehensible request! But Isaac's dad was willing to obey his heavenly Father, regardless of the message. He had acted in faith before, and he would do it again this time.

The story of Abraham's willingness to sacrifice his son is not only about the incredible tug of a dad's heart toward his child. It's also about a man who knew that obedience was more important than the potential losses incurred in the sacrifice.

The story of the Bible is filled with this principle: if you want to come into God's presence, everything else—even your most precious possession—has to be offered up to Him. A second-stringer wasn't good enough. God was so adamant about this principle that He was willing to lay His own unblemished Son on the altar.

Abraham is a great example for us. He would have wanted us to learn too that God must be first. When we hear His voice, we must obey. Nothing else really matters.

# God's Words of Life on
# PATIENCE

I wait for the LORD, my whole being waits,
>    and in his word I put my hope.
I wait for the Lord
>    more than watchmen wait for the morning.

PSALM 130:5–6

Be still before the LORD
>    and wait patiently for him.

PSALM 37:7

Everyone should be quick to listen, slow to speak and
slow to become angry.

JAMES 1:19

Patience is better than pride.

ECCLESIASTES 7:8

It is good to wait quietly
>    for the salvation of the LORD.

LAMENTATIONS 3:26

Wait for the LORD;

be strong and take heart

and wait for the LORD.

PSALM 27:14

LORD, walking in the way of your laws,

we wait for you;

your name and renown

are the desire of our hearts.

ISAIAH 26:8

Be joyful in hope, patient in affliction, faithful in prayer.

ROMANS 12:12

If we hope for what we do not yet have, we wait for it patiently.

ROMANS 8:25

See how the farmer waits for the land to yield its valuable crop, patiently waiting for the autumn and spring rains. You too, be patient and stand firm, because the Lord's coming is near.

JAMES 5:7–8

Love is patient.

1 CORINTHIANS 13:4

Be completely humble and gentle; be patient, bearing with one another in love.

EPHESIANS 4:2

[We pray] that you may live a life worthy of the Lord and please him in every way: bearing fruit in every good work, growing in the knowledge of God, being strengthened with all power according to his glorious might so that you may have great endurance and patience.

COLOSSIANS 1:10–11

Pursue righteousness, godliness, faith, love, endurance and gentleness.

1 TIMOTHY 6:11

You, Lord, are a compassionate and gracious God,
    slow to anger, abounding in love and faithfulness.

PSALM 86:15

The Lord is not slow in keeping his promise, as some understand slowness. Instead he is patient with you, not wanting anyone to perish, but everyone to come to repentance.

2 PETER 3:9

*Devotional Thought on*
# PATIENCE

Wouldn't it be great if we could read from Noah's nautical journal? Day 1 might have read, "God, You really did keep Your word. Thank You for giving me the strength to obey. Thank You for being so faithful." But day 173 may have read a bit differently: "Okay, God, I've had enough. This is the most miserable experience of my life. Are You there? Are You listening to me?"

Have you been there? Have you done something radical—moved your family to a new town or changed jobs—sincerely believing it was what God wanted you to do, only to find yourself completely miserable? I've been there too.

Well, we're in good company. Noah, Abraham, Jacob, Job: these were men who heard God's voice, believed the promise, then had to wait. And wait. And wait some more.

Are you waiting for something you thought God would have delivered by now—satisfaction at work, healing from an illness, reconciliation with a friend? The assurance we have from the Bible is that, in every case, in His own way, God's promise was good. Those who had to wait did not wait in vain. Take that promise with you today.

# God's Words of Life on
## PEACE

May the Lord of peace himself give you peace at all
times and in every way. The Lord be with all of you.

2 Thessalonians 3:16

Lord, you establish peace for us;
   all that we have accomplished you have done for us.

Isaiah 26:12

Let the peace of Christ rule in your hearts, since as
members of one body you were called to peace.

Colossians 3:15

Do not be anxious about anything, but in every
situation, by prayer and petition, with thanksgiving,
present your requests to God. And the peace of God,
which transcends all understanding, will guard your
hearts and your minds in Christ Jesus.

Philippians 4:6–7

In peace I will lie down and sleep,

    for you alone, Lord,

    make me dwell in safety.

Psalm 4:8

The Lord gives strength to his people;

    the Lord blesses his people with peace.

Psalm 29:11

You will keep in perfect peace

    those whose minds are steadfast,

    because they trust in you.

Isaiah 26:3

Great peace have those who love your law,

    and nothing can make them stumble.

Psalm 119:165

To us a child is born,

    to us a son is given,

    and the government will be on his shoulders.

And he will be called

    Wonderful Counselor, Mighty God,

    Everlasting Father, Prince of Peace.

Isaiah 9:6

Grace and peace to you from God our Father and the Lord Jesus Christ.

PHILIPPIANS 1:2

"I will make a covenant of peace with them and rid the land of savage beasts so that they may live in the wilderness and sleep in the forests in safety. I will make them and the places surrounding my hill a blessing. I will send down showers in season; there will be showers of blessing. The trees will yield their fruit and the ground will yield its crops; the people will be secure in their land. They will know that I am the LORD."

EZEKIEL 34:25–27

You know the message God sent to the people of Israel, announcing the good news of peace through Jesus Christ, who is Lord of all.

ACTS 10:36

"The LORD bless you
    and keep you;
the LORD make his face shine on you
    and be gracious to you;
the LORD turn his face toward you
    and give you peace."

NUMBERS 6:24–26

Grace and peace to you from him who is, and who was, and who is to come.

REVELATION 1:4

Love and faithfulness meet together;
> righteousness and peace kiss each other.

PSALM 85:10

This is what the LORD says:
> "I will extend peace to her like a river,
> and the wealth of nations like a flooding stream."

ISAIAH 66:12

Make every effort to keep the unity of the Spirit through the bond of peace.

EPHESIANS 4:3

If it is possible, as far as it depends on you, live at peace with everyone.

ROMANS 12:18

"Peace I leave with you; my peace I give you. I do not give to you as the world gives. Do not let your hearts be troubled and do not be afraid."

JOHN 14:27

Peacemakers who sow in peace reap a harvest of
righteousness.

JAMES 3:18

Blessed are the peacemakers,
>    for they will be called children of God.

MATTHEW 5:9

Let us therefore make every effort to do what leads to
peace and to mutual edification.

ROMANS 14:19

Submit to God and be at peace with him;
>    in this way prosperity will come to you.

JOB 22:21

The fruit of that righteousness will be peace;
>    its effect will be quietness and confidence forever.

ISAIAH 32:17

## Devotional Thought on
# PEACE

As the terminal doors slid open, I felt great. I was ready for this business trip, whatever surprises it threw my way. I felt ready and excited.

In less than sixty seconds, I was standing at the metal detectors. I loaded my small suitcase and briefcase onto the conveyor belt. Once they had disappeared into the X-ray machine, I stepped through the electronic trellis.

A security officer stopped me. "You got a computer in there?" he asked. "Uh, yes I do," I responded, trying to keep my composure. "Turn it on for me," he ordered.

Standing there, waiting for my laptop to boot up, I felt myself filling with rage. I got mad at all this airport security; I got mad at the X-ray police; I got mad at my laptop that booted up so slowly.

By the time the security checks were complete, I was furious. The peace I had felt when I entered the airport was a distant memory. I was looking for something to kick.

The next time you get derailed, take confidence in the good stuff you've put into your soul. God's holy presence is yours. He will calm you down.

# God's Words of Life on
# PLANNING

Plans fail for lack of counsel,

but with many advisers they succeed.

PROVERBS 15:22

The plans of the righteous are just.

PROVERBS 12:5

I know that you can do all things;

no purpose of yours can be thwarted.

JOB 42:2

The LORD Almighty has sworn,

"Surely, as I have planned, so it will be,

and as I have purposed, so it will happen."

ISAIAH 14:24

Those who plan what is good find love and faithfulness.

PROVERBS 14:22

The plans of the diligent lead to profit
    as surely as haste leads to poverty.

PROVERBS 21:5

The noble make noble plans,
    and by noble deeds they stand.

ISAIAH 32:8

Plans are established by seeking advice.

PROVERBS 20:18

You who say, "Today or tomorrow we will go to this or that city, spend a year there, carry on business and make money." Why, you do not even know what will happen tomorrow. What is your life? You are a mist that appears for a little while and then vanishes. Instead, you ought to say, "If it is the Lord's will, we will live and do this or that."

JAMES 4:13–15

The LORD foils the plans of the nations;
    he thwarts the purposes of the peoples.
But the plans of the LORD stand firm forever,
    the purposes of his heart through all generations.

PSALM 33:10–11

May he give you the desire of your heart
and make all your plans succeed.

PSALM 20:4

Many are the plans in a person's heart,
but it is the LORD's purpose that prevails.

PROVERBS 19:21

To humans belong the plans of the heart,
but from the LORD comes the proper answer of the
tongue.
All a person's ways seem pure to them,
but motives are weighed by the LORD.
Commit to the LORD whatever you do,
and he will establish your plans.

PROVERBS 16:1–3

There is no wisdom, no insight, no plan
that can succeed against the LORD.

PROVERBS 21:30

## *Devotional Thought on*
# PLANNING

Most men I know carry some kind of calendar. The one I carry is huge. It includes pockets for my driver's license and credit cards along with monthly and daily calendars. This is sound planning, wouldn't you agree? Come to think of it, it's pretty presumptuous too.

Although King Solomon never carried a planner or attended a time-management seminar, he certainly understood all of these things. "Do not boast about tomorrow, for you do not know what a day may bring," he wisely said (Proverbs 27:1).

My grandmother took this exhortation seriously. She never talked about future plans without prefacing them with "The Lord willing." "The Lord willing, we'll have roasted chicken for dinner." "The Lord willing, we'll go to the store tomorrow." "The Lord willing, we'll see you this summer."

Carrying a calendar is good. Planning is a wise use of your time. Knowing what's coming next week, next month, and next year makes a lot of sense. But be sure to write this stuff in pencil, and be careful about being too confident. The Lord willing, we'll get to tomorrow.

# God's Words of Life on
## POWER

"With God all things are possible."

MATTHEW 19:26

"I am the LORD, the God of all mankind. Is anything too hard for me?"

JEREMIAH 32:27

The LORD is slow to anger but great in power;
the LORD will not leave the guilty unpunished.
His way is in the whirlwind and the storm,
and clouds are the dust of his feet.

NAHUM 1:3

All the peoples of the earth
are regarded as nothing.
He does as he pleases
with the powers of heaven
and the peoples of the earth.
No one can hold back his hand
or say to him: "What have you done?"

DANIEL 4:35

You, God, are awesome in your sanctuary;

the God of Israel gives power and strength to his people.

Praise be to God!

Psalm 68:35

Your strength will equal your days.

Deuteronomy 33:25

"I will strengthen them in the Lord

and in his name they will live securely,"

declares the Lord.

Zechariah 10:12

[We pray] that you may live a life worthy of the Lord and please him in every way: bearing fruit in every good work, growing in the knowledge of God, being strengthened with all power according to his glorious might so that you may have great endurance and patience.

Colossians 1:10–11

He has made everything beautiful in its time. He has also set eternity in the human heart; yet no one can fathom what God has done from beginning to end.

Ecclesiastes 3:11

He spreads out the northern skies over empty space;
     he suspends the earth over nothing.
He wraps up the waters in his clouds,
     yet the clouds do not burst under their weight.
He covers the face of the full moon,
     spreading his clouds over it.
He marks out the horizon on the face of the waters
     for a boundary between light and darkness. . . .
By his breath the skies became fair;
     his hand pierced the gliding serpent.
And these are but the outer fringe of his works;
     how faint the whisper we hear of him!
     Who then can understand the thunder of his
          power?

JOB 26:7–10, 13–14

[God's] wisdom is profound, his power is vast.
     Who has resisted him and come out unscathed?

JOB 9:4

Your arm is endowed with power;
     your hand is strong, your right hand exalted.

PSALM 89:13

Be strong in the Lord and in his mighty power.

EPHESIANS 6:10

Your right hand, LORD,
    was majestic in power.
Your right hand, LORD,
    shattered the enemy.

EXODUS 15:6

Yours, LORD, is the greatness and the power
    and the glory and the majesty and the splendor,
    for everything in heaven and earth is yours.
Yours, LORD, is the kingdom;
    you are exalted as head over all.
Wealth and honor come from you;
    you are the ruler of all things.
In your hands are strength and power
    to exalt and give strength to all.
Now, our God, we give you thanks,
    and praise your glorious name.

1 CHRONICLES 29:11–13

As for me, I am filled with power,
    with the Spirit of the LORD,
    and with justice and might.

MICAH 3:8

I pray that out of his glorious riches he may strengthen you with power through his Spirit in your inner being, so that Christ may dwell in your hearts through faith. And I pray that you, being rooted and established in love, may have power, together with all the Lord's holy people, to grasp how wide and long and high and deep is the love of Christ.

EPHESIANS 3:16–18

"You will receive power when the Holy Spirit comes on you; and you will be my witnesses in Jerusalem, and in all Judea and Samaria, and to the ends of the earth."

ACTS 1:8

You may say to yourself, "My power and the strength of my hands have produced this wealth for me." But remember the LORD your God, for it is he who gives you the ability to produce wealth, and so confirms his covenant."

DEUTERONOMY 8:17–18

"Not by might nor by power, but by my Spirit," says the LORD Almighty.

ZECHARIAH 4:6

*Devotional Thought on*

# POWER

How fast will your car go? You don't know? Well, how high do the numbers on your speedometer go—130 . . . 140 . . . 150? And you've probably never even approached 100. Right? Wow, just think of all that raw, unused power!

If you're mechanically inclined, you know something about this power. You know that if you actually drove at those speeds often, you could seriously damage your engine.

In your job as a dad, you have a high-powered disciplinary engine with its own imaginary speedometer. This instrument registers numbers much higher than posted and safe speed limits. Do you have the right to push your accelerator to the floor and demonstrate some of that power? Of course you do. But most experts agree that if you spend too much time at those high speeds, you'll do harm.

Sometimes dads are called upon to use their power. Yet it's usually better to leave some of that force unused.

God's restraint—His mercy and His grace—is what makes Him so awesome. His tenderness and patience melt our defiance and realign our wayward hearts.

Perhaps you need to discover the power of unused power. Your family will be grateful.

# God's Words of Life on
# PRAYER

"Before they call I will answer;

while they are still speaking I will hear."

Isaiah 65:24

"Ask and it will be given to you; seek and you will find; knock and the door will be opened to you. For everyone who asks receives; the one who seeks finds; and to the one who knocks, the door will be opened."

Matthew 7:7–8

"Truly I tell you that if two of you on earth agree about anything they ask for, it will be done for them by my Father in heaven. For where two or three gather in my name, there am I with them."

Matthew 18:19–20

Dear friends, if our hearts do not condemn us, we have confidence before God and receive from him anything we ask, because we keep his commands and do what pleases him.

1 John 3:21–22

Pray continually.

1 Thessalonians 5:17

The Lord is near to all who call on him,
    to all who call on him in truth.

Psalm 145:18

I call to God,
    and the Lord saves me.
Evening, morning and noon
    I cry out in distress,
    and he hears my voice.

Psalm 55:16–17

When you pray, go into your room, close the door and
pray to your Father, who is unseen. Then your Father,
who sees what is done in secret, will reward you.

Matthew 6:6

Devote yourselves to prayer, being watchful and thankful.

Colossians 4:2

"You will call on me and come and pray to me, and I
will listen to you. You will seek me and find me when
you seek me with all your heart. I will be found by you,"
declares the Lord.

Jeremiah 29:12–14

We have not stopped praying for you. We continually ask God to fill you with the knowledge of his will through all the wisdom and understanding that the Spirit gives.

COLOSSIANS 1:9

Pray in the Spirit on all occasions with all kinds of prayers and requests. With this in mind, be alert and always keep on praying for all the Lord's people.

EPHESIANS 6:18

Let all the faithful pray to you
while you may be found;
surely the rising of the mighty waters
will not reach them.

PSALM 32:6

Hear me, LORD, my plea is just;
listen to my cry.
Hear my prayer—
it does not rise from deceitful lips.

PSALM 17:1

The LORD has heard my cry for mercy;
the LORD accepts my prayer.

PSALM 6:9

"Call to me and I will answer you and tell you great and unsearchable things you do not know."

JEREMIAH 33:3

"Because he loves me," says the LORD, "I will rescue him;
I will protect him, for he acknowledges my name.
He will call on me, and I will answer him;
I will be with him in trouble,
I will deliver him and honor him."

PSALM 91:14–15

The LORD is far from the wicked,
but he hears the prayer of the righteous.

PROVERBS 15:29

Take delight in the LORD,
and he will give you the desires of your heart.

PSALM 37:4

Let us . . . approach God's throne of grace with confidence, so that we may receive mercy and find grace to help us in our time of need.

HEBREWS 4:16

The eyes of the Lord are on the righteous
and his ears are attentive to their prayer.

1 PETER 3:12

"Very truly I tell you, my Father will give you whatever you ask in my name. Until now you have not asked for anything in my name. Ask and you will receive, and your joy will be complete."

JOHN 16:23–24

"If my people, who are called by my name, will humble themselves and pray and seek my face and turn from their wicked ways, then I will hear from heaven, and I will forgive their sin and will heal their land."

2 CHRONICLES 7:14

## Devotional Thought on
# PRAYER

God spoke about Job to Satan, saying, "There is no one on earth like him; he is blameless and upright, a man who fears God and shuns evil" (Job 1:8). Perhaps one of the things that so impressed God about this man was the way he faithfully prayed for his children. How often do your children see you face the altar and plead their case? "Father in heaven, please protect Missy today in school. Guard her mind and her actions. Talk to her through her friends who love You, and keep her from those who would turn her away from Your love."

As Missy hears her dad hold her up before the throne of God, the chills run down her spine. *My dad is praying for me.* These words will roll over again and again in her mind. Over the course of the years, these prayers could change her life.

Pray for your children. Lift them up before the Father and seek His protection and blessing on their lives. This will be a powerful thing—both for you and for them.

# God's Words of Life on
# PRIORITIES

Since we are surrounded by such a great cloud of witnesses, let us throw off everything that hinders and the sin that so easily entangles. And let us run with perseverance the race marked out for us, fixing our eyes on Jesus, the pioneer and perfecter of faith. For the joy set before him he endured the cross, scorning its shame, and sat down at the right hand of the throne of God.

HEBREWS 12:1–2

Someone will say, "You have faith; I have deeds." Show me your faith without deeds, and I will show you my faith by my deeds.

JAMES 2:18

"This, then, is how you should pray:

"Our Father in heaven,

hallowed be your name,

your kingdom come,

your will be done,

on earth as it is in heaven.'"

MATTHEW 6:9–10

Make my joy complete by being like-minded, having the same love, being one in spirit and of one mind. Do nothing out of selfish ambition or vain conceit. Rather, in humility value others above yourselves, not looking to your own interests but each of you to the interests of the others. In your relationships with one another, have the same mindset as Christ Jesus.

PHILIPPIANS 2:2–5

Whatever were gains to me I now consider loss for the sake of Christ. What is more, I consider everything a loss because of the surpassing worth of knowing Christ Jesus my Lord, for whose sake I have lost all things. I consider them garbage, that I may gain Christ.

PHILIPPIANS 3:7–8

I consider my life worth nothing to me; my only aim is to finish the race and complete the task the Lord Jesus has given me—the task of testifying to the good news of God's grace.

ACTS 20:24

"Do not worry, saying, 'What shall we eat?' or 'What shall we drink?' or 'What shall we wear?' . . . Seek first his kingdom and his righteousness, and all these things will be given to you as well."

MATTHEW 6:31, 33

"I tell you, use worldly wealth to gain friends for yourselves, so that when it is gone, you will be welcomed into eternal dwellings. Whoever can be trusted with very little can also be trusted with much, and whoever is dishonest with very little will also be dishonest with much. So if you have not been trustworthy in handling worldly wealth, who will trust you with true riches?"

Luke 16:9–11

Blessed is the one
    who does not walk in step with the wicked
or stand in the way that sinners take
    or sit in the company of mockers,
but whose delight is in the law of the Lord,
    and who meditates on his law day and night.

Psalm 1:1–2

Whatever you do, work at it with all your heart, as working for the Lord, not for human masters, since you know that you will receive an inheritance from the Lord as a reward. It is the Lord Christ you are serving.

Colossians 3:23–24

*Devotional Thought on*
# PRIORITIES

I am a card-carrying acrophobic; I'm desperately afraid of heights.

I was building a house with my Sunday school class. Since I'm fairly adept at driving nails, I had volunteered to climb up to the top of the first-floor framed walls to secure them. When I had completed one section, I stood to walk across the three-and-a-half-inch-wide "walkway" to the other side of the house. Suddenly, my legs froze. I could feel the pounding of my heart from my fingertips to my baseball cap. This was not funny.

Without looking up or down, I slowly reached my arms straight out from my sides and began to walk . . . one treacherous step at a time. Halfway across, I realized that my outstretched arms were providing the perfect antidote for my fear—they were giving me balance.

Being successful at work, effectively fathering your kids, keeping your exercise and diet routine intact, spending enough time with your wife, being disciplined in your spiritual life: all of this can create such anxiety that you feel frozen, unable to walk across the high wall. How does one achieve balance in life?

Throughout His life Jesus kept His priorities in order. He refused to allow the stress and pressure of any one of the obligations of life to overshadow the others. Then one dark Friday afternoon, our Savior spread out His arms and gave His life for you and me. His provision of grace provided us with the luxury of living our lives in perfect balance—unencumbered by the relentless pressures of life. Isn't this incredible?

# God's Words of Life on
## SELF-CONTROL

You desired faithfulness even in the womb;
you taught me wisdom in that secret place.

PSALM 51:6

The world and its desires pass away, but whoever does the will of God lives forever.

1 JOHN 2:17

The mind governed by the Spirit is life and peace.

ROMANS 8:6

Do your best to present yourself to God as one approved, a worker who does not need to be ashamed.

2 TIMOTHY 2:15

The fruit of that righteousness will be peace;
its effect will be quietness and confidence forever.

ISAIAH 32:17

"Whoever finds their life will lose it, and whoever loses their life for my sake will find it."

MATTHEW 10:39

You will keep in perfect peace

   those whose minds are steadfast,

   because they trust in you.

ISAIAH 26:3

The kingdom of God is not a matter of eating and drinking, but of righteousness, peace and joy in the Holy Spirit.

ROMANS 14:17

Since . . . you have been raised with Christ, set your hearts on things above, where Christ is, seated at the right hand of God. Set your minds on things above, not on earthly things.

COLOSSIANS 3:1–2

Be careful, and watch yourselves closely so that you do not forget the things your eyes have seen or let them fade from your heart as long as you live. Teach them to your children and to their children after them.

DEUTERONOMY 4:9

This is my prayer: that your love may abound more and more in knowledge and depth of insight, so that you may be able to discern what is best and may be pure and blameless for the day of Christ.

PHILIPPIANS 1:9–10

Let your eyes look straight ahead,
  fix your gaze directly before you.
Give careful thought to the paths for your feet
  and be steadfast in all your ways.
Do not turn to the right or the left;
  keep your foot from evil.

PROVERBS 4:25–27

He follows my decrees
  and faithfully keeps my laws.
That man is righteous;
  he will surely live,
  declares the Sovereign LORD.

EZEKIEL 18:9

The grace of God has appeared that offers salvation to all people. It teaches us to say "No" to ungodliness and worldly passions, and to live self-controlled, upright and godly lives in this present age.

TITUS 2:11–12

*Devotional Thought on*
## SELF-CONTROL

Exodus 20–23 contains a list of pretty tough rules for the Israelites to follow. I'm sure listening to this list was as stressful to these people as getting ready for finals in school was for us. As we're getting down toward the end of the list of laws, we bump into something quite simple—and powerful. Something that sounds as if it could have been written for my college experience: "Do not follow the crowd in doing wrong" (Exodus 23:2).

As adults, we feel the pull toward doing wrong because our entire culture seems to be doing it—shaving the truth just a bit, saying regretful things, the temptation toward moral failure. It's pretty overwhelming. And of course our children face this terrible temptation as well.

So what's the Bible's persuasive advice for this dilemma? It's a simple "don't." No explanation necessary. Just "don't." The writer of these words knew what we know: following a crowd to do wrong things is stupid. Set an example for your family and stand for what you know is right. Encourage your kids to do the same. You'll both be so happy you did.

# God's Words of Life on
# SERVANTHOOD

"Whoever wants to become great among you must be your servant, and whoever wants to be first must be slave of all."

MARK 10:43–44

Though I am free and belong to no one, I have made myself a slave to everyone, to win as many as possible. To the Jews I became like a Jew, to win the Jews. To those under the law I became like one under the law (though I myself am not under the law), so as to win those under the law. To those not having the law I became like one not having the law (though I am not free from God's law but am under Christ's law), so as to win those not having the law. To the weak I became weak, to win the weak. I have become all things to all people so that by all possible means I might save some.

1 CORINTHIANS 9:19–22

Serve one another humbly in love.

GALATIANS 5:13

In your relationships with one another, have the same mindset as Christ Jesus:

> Who, being in very nature God,
>> did not consider equality with God something
>>> to be used to his own advantage;
> rather, he made himself nothing
>> by taking the very nature of a servant,
>> being made in human likeness.
> And being found in appearance as a man,
>> he humbled himself
>> by becoming obedient to death—
>> even death on a cross!

PHILIPPIANS 2:5–8

"Whoever wants to save their life will lose it, but whoever loses their life for me will find it."

MATTHEW 16:25

If serving the LORD seems undesirable to you, then choose for yourselves this day whom you will serve. . . . But as for me and my household, we will serve the LORD.

JOSHUA 24:15

Be sure to fear the LORD and serve him faithfully with all your heart; consider what great things he has done for you.

1 SAMUEL 12:24

Be devoted to one another in love. Honor one another above yourselves. Never be lacking in zeal, but keep your spiritual fervor, serving the Lord.

Romans 12:10–11

What does the Lord your God ask of you but to fear the Lord your God, to walk in obedience to him, to love him, to serve the Lord your God with all your heart and with all your soul, and to observe the Lord's commands and decrees?

Deuteronomy 10:12–13

"Whoever welcomes this little child in my name welcomes me; and whoever welcomes me welcomes the one who sent me. For it is the one who is least among you all who is the greatest."

Luke 9:48

If anyone serves, they should do so with the strength God provides, so that in all things God may be praised through Jesus Christ. To him be the glory and the power for ever and ever. Amen.

1 Peter 4:11

## Devotional Thought on
# SERVANTHOOD

The setting of the Last Supper was very informal, contrary to the many artists' renditions of the scene. These men were celebrating the Passover in the traditional way, reclining on the floor.

Suddenly Jesus stood up, took off His outer robe, tied a towel around His waist, poured water into a basin, and began washing His disciples' filthy feet. Here was the long-hoped-for Messiah, the Savior of mankind, on His knees, rinsing road dirt. *Where's the houseboy?* they must have thought. *Jesus shouldn't be doing this!*

So what was Jesus doing? What was He saying in this moment of subservient humility? Love requires humility—power demands service.

Do we want respect at home? Of course we do. Do we want to own up to our responsibility as the heads of our homes? Absolutely. Then we have to trade in our professional uniform for a work shirt, our crown for a basin, our robe for a towel. We're going to have to get off our high horse and get on our knees. Confessing. Washing. Forgiving. Serving. Jesus' example on this unforgettable night ought to be enough.

# God's Words of Life on
# SPIRITUAL GROWTH

Forgetting what is behind and straining toward what is ahead, I press on toward the goal to win the prize for which God has called me heavenward in Christ Jesus.

PHILIPPIANS 3:13–14

"Whoever believes in me, as Scripture has said, rivers of living water will flow from within them."

JOHN 7:38

We will no longer be infants, tossed back and forth by the waves, and blown here and there by every wind of teaching and by the cunning and craftiness of people in their deceitful scheming. Instead, speaking the truth in love, we will grow to become in every respect the mature body of him who is the head, that is, Christ. From him the whole body, joined and held together by every supporting ligament, grows and builds itself up in love, as each part does its work.

EPHESIANS 4:14–16

The fruit of the Spirit is love, joy, peace, forbearance, kindness, goodness, faithfulness, gentleness and self-control. Against such things there is no law. Those who belong to Christ Jesus have crucified the flesh with its passions and desires. Since we live by the Spirit, let us keep in step with the Spirit.

GALATIANS 5:22–25

Those who live in accordance with the Spirit have their minds set on what the Spirit desires.

ROMANS 8:5

"A time is coming and has now come when the true worshipers will worship the Father in the Spirit and in truth, for they are the kind of worshipers the Father seeks. God is spirit, and his worshipers must worship in the Spirit and in truth."

JOHN 4:23–24

I urge you, brothers and sisters, in view of God's mercy, to offer your bodies as a living sacrifice, holy and pleasing to God—this is your true and proper worship.

ROMANS 12:1

Like newborn babies, crave pure spiritual milk, so that by it you may grow up in your salvation, now that you have tasted that the Lord is good.

1 PETER 2:2–3

Since we are receiving a kingdom that cannot be shaken, let us be thankful, and so worship God acceptably with reverence and awe.

HEBREWS 12:28

Cause me to understand the way of your precepts,
    that I may meditate on your wonderful deeds.

PSALM 119:27

Grow in the grace and knowledge of our Lord and Savior Jesus Christ. To him be glory both now and forever!

2 PETER 3:18

*Devotional Thought on*

# SPIRITUAL GROWTH

When I was in grade school, Memorial Day was my favorite holiday because I played in the marching band, and school was almost over for the whole summer. Now that I'm older, I still have a deep love for the day . . . but for different reasons. It's humbling to realize that people—total strangers—spilled their blood for me.

God's people had a similar event in their tradition. God's promises had been so visible to the Jews that, every year, they set a week aside to remember and be grateful. This Jewish tradition has a very, very important lesson to teach dads: you are the priest in your home. Tell your children about God's faithfulness. Introduce your loved ones to God's amazing grace. Bring your family to their own personal experience of saving faith.

We have no choice but to live our lives as an example. We must teach our children God's ways, remind them of His faithfulness, and show them His grace.

# God's Words of Life on
# STRENGTH

The LORD gives strength to his people;
>    the LORD blesses his people with peace.

PSALM 29:11

"I will strengthen them in the LORD
>    and in his name they will live securely,"
>    declares the LORD.

ZECHARIAH 10:12

[We pray] that you may live a life worthy of the Lord
and please him in every way: bearing fruit in every
good work, growing in the knowledge of God, being
strengthened with all power according to his glorious
might so that you may have great endurance and patience.

COLOSSIANS 1:10–11

You, God, are awesome in your sanctuary;
>    the God of Israel gives power and strength
>    to his people.
Praise be to God!

PSALM 68:35

Even youths grow tired and weary,
and young men stumble and fall;
but those who hope in the LORD
will renew their strength.
They will soar on wings like eagles;
they will run and not grow weary,
they will walk and not be faint.

ISAIAH 40:30–31

[The Lord] said to me, "My grace is sufficient for you, for my power is made perfect in weakness." Therefore I will boast all the more gladly about my weaknesses, so that Christ's power may rest on me. That is why, for Christ's sake, I delight in weaknesses, in insults, in hardships, in persecutions, in difficulties. For when I am weak, then I am strong.

2 CORINTHIANS 12:9–10

The LORD is the strength of his people,
a fortress of salvation for his anointed one.

PSALM 28:8

"In the LORD alone
are deliverance and strength."

ISAIAH 45:24

Be strong in the Lord and in his mighty power.

EPHESIANS 6:10

He gives strength to the weary
and increases the power of the weak.

ISAIAH 40:29

I pray that out of his glorious riches he may strengthen you with power through his Spirit in your inner being.

EPHESIANS 3:16

"I will strengthen you and help you;
I will uphold you with my righteous right hand."

ISAIAH 41:10

I can do all this through him who gives me strength.

PHILIPPIANS 4:13

The eyes of the LORD range throughout the earth to strengthen those whose hearts are fully committed to him.

2 CHRONICLES 16:9

## *Devotional Thought on*
# STRENGTH

You can't play a cassette in a compact disc player. If you want a certain result, you're going to have to be plugged into the right source.

Being a man who lives in such a way that your friends and your family are actually blessed because of your life is a very tall order. In fact, Jesus was quick to say that if we're not connected to Him, our "fruit" will be worthless and our "branch" will die (John 15). And dead branches are good only for bonfires.

This principle isn't very deep. We all know that if we're not connecting ourselves to the right stuff, our disobedient lives will show it. We can't expect to fill our lives with sin and have others see purity and righteousness. As computer programmers sometimes say, "Garbage in, garbage out."

If, in the quietness of your own heart, you know you've got a problem that others can, could, or will see, check which source you're connected to. "Apart from me you can do nothing," Jesus said (John 15:5).

# God's Words of Life on
# STRESS

"Come to me, all you who are weary and burdened,
and I will give you rest. Take my yoke upon you
and learn from me, for I am gentle and humble
in heart, and you will find rest for your souls.
For my yoke is easy and my burden is light."

MATTHEW 11:28–30

When I am in distress, I call to you,
because you answer me.

PSALM 86:7

Cast your cares on the LORD
and he will sustain you;
he will never let
the righteous be shaken.

PSALM 55:22

Be merciful to me, LORD, for I am in distress;
my eyes grow weak with sorrow,
my soul and body with grief.

PSALM 31:9

In my distress I called to the Lord;
 I called out to my God.
From his temple he heard my voice;
 my cry came to his ears.

2 Samuel 22:7

When you pass through the waters,
 I will be with you;
and when you pass through the rivers,
 they will not sweep over you.
When you walk through the fire,
 you will not be burned;
 the flames will not set you ablaze.
For I am the Lord your God.

Isaiah 43:2–3

You will keep in perfect peace
 those whose minds are steadfast,
 because they trust in you.
Trust in the Lord forever,
 for the Lord, the Lord himself, is the Rock eternal.

Isaiah 26:3–4

I will listen to what God the Lord says;
 he promises peace to his people.

Psalm 85:8

In my distress I called to the LORD;
  I cried to my God for help.
From his temple he heard my voice;
  my cry came before him, into his ears.

PSALM 18:6

When God gives someone wealth and possessions, and the ability to enjoy them, to accept their lot and be happy in their toil—this is a gift of God. They seldom reflect on the days of their life, because God keeps them occupied with gladness of heart.

ECCLESIASTES 5:19–20

Since we have been justified through faith, we have peace with God through our Lord Jesus Christ, through whom we have gained access by faith into this grace in which we now stand. And we boast in the hope of the glory of God.

ROMANS 5:1–2

This is what the Sovereign LORD, the Holy One of Israel, says:
  "In repentance and rest is your salvation,
  in quietness and trust is your strength."

ISAIAH 30:15

"I will refresh the weary and satisfy the faint."

JEREMIAH 31:25

Because so many people were coming and going that [the apostles] did not even have a chance to eat, [Jesus] said to them, "Come with me by yourselves to a quiet place and get some rest."

MARK 6:31

"Remember the Sabbath day by keeping it holy. Six days you shall labor and do all your work, but the seventh day is a sabbath to the LORD your God. On it you shall not do any work, neither you, nor your son or daughter. . . . For in six days the LORD made the heavens and the earth, the sea, and all that is in them, but he rested on the seventh day. Therefore the LORD blessed the Sabbath day and made it holy."

EXODUS 20:8–11

He makes me lie down in green pastures,
he leads me beside quiet waters,
he refreshes my soul.
He guides me along the right paths
for his name's sake.

PSALM 23:2–3

"Do not let your hearts be troubled. You believe in God; believe also in me."

JOHN 14:1

Let us not become weary in doing good, for at the proper time we will reap a harvest if we do not give up.

Galatians 6:9

Consider it pure joy, my brothers and sisters, whenever you face trials of many kinds, because you know that the testing of your faith produces perseverance. Let perseverance finish its work so that you may be mature and complete, not lacking anything.

James 1:2–4

## Devotional Thought on
# STRESS

Have you ever been completely frozen? I'm not talking about the kind of frozen that happens when a subzero windchill cuts through your warmest winter clothing, or the kind of frozen that happens when your engine oil reservoir runs dry. I'm talking about the frozen that comes when stress and pressure bring you to the breaking point.

Sometimes the circumstances of life stop us cold. Sometimes family pressures and work stress leave us frozen in our tracks, completely unable to move. But when we have completely run out of answers, when our solutions are woefully inadequate, when our energy and our desire to go on have vanished, God's Holy Spirit picks up the phone on the first ring. "Love, joy, peace, forbearance, kindness, goodness, faithfulness, gentleness and self-control" (Galatians 5:22–23) are then ours for the asking.

Let the sovereign God of the universe thaw your cold heart. Let His grace free your aching soul. Be filled with His Spirit . . . He'll deliver you. That's a promise.

# God's Words of Life on
# SUCCESS

"Be strong and very courageous. Be careful to obey
all the law my servant Moses gave you; do not turn
from it to the right or to the left, that you may be
successful wherever you go. Keep this Book of the
Law always on your lips; meditate on it day and night,
so that you may be careful to do everything written
in it. Then you will be prosperous and successful."

JOSHUA 1:7–8

[King Uzziah] sought God during the days of Zechariah,
who instructed him in the fear of God. As long as he
sought the LORD, God gave him success.

2 CHRONICLES 26:5

When his master saw that the LORD was with him and
that the LORD gave him success in everything he did,
Joseph found favor in his eyes and became his attendant.
Potiphar put him in charge of his household, and he
entrusted to his care everything he owned.

GENESIS 39:3–4

Hezekiah trusted in the Lord, the God of Israel. There was no one like him among all the kings of Judah, either before him or after him. He held fast to the Lord and did not stop following him; he kept the commands the Lord had given Moses. And the Lord was with him; he was successful in whatever he undertook.

2 Kings 18:5–7

Blessed is the one
    who does not walk in step with the wicked
or stand in the way that sinners take
    or sit in the company of mockers,
but whose delight is in the law of the Lord,
    and who meditates on his law day and night.
That person is like a tree planted by streams of water,
    which yields its fruit in season
and whose leaf does not wither—
    whatever they do prospers.

Psalm 1:1–3

Have faith in the Lord your God and you will be upheld; have faith in his prophets and you will be successful.

2 Chronicles 20:20

In everything that [King Hezekiah] undertook in the service of God's temple and in obedience to the law and the commands, he sought his God and worked wholeheartedly. And so he prospered.

2 Chronicles 31:21

Commit to the Lord whatever you do,
and he will establish your plans.

Proverbs 16:3

May he give you the desire of your heart
and make all your plans succeed.
May we shout for joy over your victory
and lift up our banners in the name of our God.
May the Lord grant all your requests.

Psalm 20:4–5

Plans fail for lack of counsel,
but with many advisers they succeed.

Proverbs 15:22

## Devotional Thought on
# SUCCESS

Let's take a little journey back to geometry class. We're going to discuss postulates. For an example, let's try a family postulate. If I am married and my wife gives birth to a baby, then I am a father. If I make a rule and my child disobeys me, then I have some disciplining work to do. Since the first part of each statement is true, and since the second part of each statement is also true, then the combination of the first and second parts makes each conclusion true for sure. See how these work?

In Deuteronomy 30 we have an amazing postulate. It starts with verse 1 and ends with verse 3. Moses presented this message to the Israelites in terms they could clearly understand: since God can be taken at His word, if He finds you obedient to His law, then He will "restore your fortunes and have compassion on you" (v. 3).

While theologians will arm-wrestle over the kind of "prosperity" God is referring to here, it's indisputable that He does promise the kind of success that is consistent within His economy—where a foreign import can be bought with lunch money and where a happy family is a priceless treasure.

# God's Words of Life on
# THANKFULNESS

Praise the LORD.

Give thanks to the LORD, for he is good;

    his love endures forever.

PSALM 106:1

I will extol the LORD at all times;

    his praise will always be on my lips.

PSALM 34:1

By prayer and petition, with thanksgiving, present your requests to God.

PHILIPPIANS 4:6

Give thanks in all circumstances; for this is God's will for you in Christ Jesus.

1 THESSALONIANS 5:18

Thanks be to God! He gives us the victory through our Lord Jesus Christ.

1 CORINTHIANS 15:57

I will give thanks to the LORD because of his righteousness;

> I will sing the praises of the name of the LORD Most
> High.

PSALM 7:17

Just as you received Christ Jesus as Lord, continue to live your lives in him, rooted and built up in him, strengthened in the faith as you were taught, and overflowing with thankfulness.

COLOSSIANS 2:6–7

Thanks be to God, who always leads us as captives in Christ's triumphal procession and uses us to spread the aroma of the knowledge of him everywhere.

2 CORINTHIANS 2:14

Let them give thanks to the LORD for his unfailing love

> and his wonderful deeds for mankind.

PSALM 107:21

You turned my wailing into dancing;

> you removed my sackcloth and clothed me with joy,

that my heart may sing your praises and not be silent.

> LORD my God, I will praise you forever.

PSALM 30:11–12

Enter his gates with thanksgiving
and his courts with praise;
give thanks to him and praise his name.

Psalm 100:4

Come, let us sing for joy to the Lord;
let us shout aloud to the Rock of our salvation.
Let us come before him with thanksgiving
and extol him with music and song.

Psalm 95:1–2

Thanks be to God for his indescribable gift!

2 Corinthians 9:15

Let the peace of Christ rule in your hearts, since as members of one body you were called to peace. And be thankful. Let the message of Christ dwell among you richly as you teach and admonish one another with all wisdom through psalms, hymns, and songs from the Spirit, singing to God with gratitude in your hearts. And whatever you do, whether in word or deed, do it all in the name of the Lord Jesus, giving thanks to God the Father through him.

Colossians 3:15–17

I will extol the LORD with all my heart

    in the council of the upright and in the assembly.

Great are the works of the LORD;

    they are pondered by all who delight in them.

PSALM 111:1–2

*Devotional Thought on*

# THANKFULNESS

There has always been something very unusual about Billy Webb. It took me a while to figure out what was so special about this particular friend.

Then one day it hit me. Billy is a handwritten-thank-you-note man. From the very first time we met for lunch until our most recent outing, I've received a note in the mail a few days later from him. These notes are not long and drawn-out; in fact, they usually fit on one side of a four-by-six card. But even when he has picked up the tab for lunch, Billy thanks me for my time and for my friendship.

The apostle Paul opened nearly every one of his thirteen New Testament letters with a "thank you." The letter to the church in Philippi is especially strong. "I thank my God every time I remember you. In all my prayers for all of you, I always pray with joy because of your partnership in the gospel," he wrote (Philippians 1:3–5).

Are you a thank-you-note man in the lives of your children, family, and friends? Being such a man takes only a moment, but the dividends are astonishing. Try it. You'll see.

# God's Words of Life on
# TRUST

Those who know your name trust in you,
>for you, LORD, have never forsaken those who
>seek you.

PSALM 9:10

Those who trust in the LORD are like Mount Zion,
>which cannot be shaken but endures forever.

PSALM 125:1

It is better to take refuge in the LORD
>than to trust in humans.
It is better to take refuge in the LORD
>than to trust in princes.

PSALM 118:8–9

Why, my soul, are you downcast?
>Why so disturbed within me?
Put your hope in God,
>for I will yet praise him,
>my Savior and my God.

PSALM 42:5

Blessed are those whose help is the God of Jacob,
whose hope is in the Lord their God.

Psalm 146:5

Whoever gives heed to instruction prospers,
and blessed is the one who trusts in the Lord.

Proverbs 16:20

"Blessed is the one who trusts in the Lord,
whose confidence is in him.
They will be like a tree planted by the water
that sends out its roots by the stream.
It does not fear when heat comes;
its leaves are always green.
It has no worries in a year of drought
and never fails to bear fruit."

Jeremiah 17:7–8

Trust in the Lord and do good;
dwell in the land and enjoy safe pasture.

Psalm 37:3

Those who trust in the Lord will prosper.

Proverbs 28:25

Anyone who believes in [Jesus] will never be put to shame.

Romans 10:11

Nebuchadnezzar said, "Praise be to the God of Shadrach, Meshach and Abednego, who has sent his angel and rescued his servants! They trusted in him and defied the king's command and were willing to give up their lives rather than serve or worship any god except their own God."

DANIEL 3:28

Fear of man will prove to be a snare,
    but whoever trusts in the LORD is kept safe.

PROVERBS 29:25

Trust in the LORD with all your heart
    and lean not on your own understanding.

PROVERBS 3:5

Be strong and take heart,
    all you who hope in the LORD.

PSALM 31:24

The LORD is good,
    a refuge in times of trouble.
He cares for those who trust in him.

NAHUM 1:7

## Devotional Thought on
# TRUST

Our family had flown to Southern California. At exactly three thirty the next morning, I woke up to something I'd never heard before. It was a cracking sound, reminiscent of lifting a sticking window sash. And then, incredibly, our hotel room began to roll. Earthquake! When we saw the news later that morning, we saw freeways—the very ones we had traveled only hours before—twisted and broken.

As I watched the local news shows and listened to the trembling voices of the victims, I learned that property damage and the lack of warning are not the worst parts of living through these natural disasters. No, the greatest ruin an earthquake delivers is in the hearts of people who can no longer count on the dependability of solid ground. Terra firma loses its firma.

What can you count on . . . your job, your cat, your Maytag? How about your stock portfolio? Your relationships? Your health?

None of these things is worthy of our absolute trust. Incredible as it may sound, they will all let us down. But trusting in God will never bring disappointment. He is enough. His reliability is legendary. His faithfulness is completely sure . . . absolutely firma.

# God's Words of Life on
# VALUES

One person gives freely, yet gains even more;

    another withholds unduly, but comes to poverty.

PROVERBS 11:24

"If you do good to those who are good to you, what credit is that to you? Even sinners do that. And if you lend to those from whom you expect repayment, what credit is that to you? Even sinners lend to sinners, expecting to be repaid in full. But love your enemies, do good to them, and lend to them without expecting to get anything back. Then your reward will be great, and you will be children of the Most High. . . . Be merciful, just as your Father is merciful."

LUKE 6:33–36

What does the LORD require of you?

To act justly and to love mercy

    and to walk humbly with your God.

MICAH 6:8

Who may ascend the mountain of the LORD?
>   Who may stand in his holy place?
The one who has clean hands and a pure heart,
>   who does not trust in an idol
>   or swear by a false god.
They will receive blessing from the LORD
>   and vindication from God their Savior.

PSALM 24:3–5

Give me only my daily bread.
Otherwise, I may have too much and disown you
>   and say, "Who is the LORD?"
Or I may become poor and steal,
>   and so dishonor the name of my God.

PROVERBS 30:8–9

Jesus replied: "'Love the Lord your God with all your heart and with all your soul and with all your mind.' This is the first and greatest commandment. And the second is like it: 'Love your neighbor as yourself.'"

MATTHEW 22:37–39

"Do to others as you would have them do to you."

LUKE 6:31

Speak and act as those who are going to be judged by the law that gives freedom, because judgment without mercy will be shown to anyone who has not been merciful. Mercy triumphs over judgment.

James 2:12–13

Be careful that you do not forget the Lord your God, failing to observe his commands, his laws and his decrees. . . . Otherwise, when you eat and are satisfied, when you build fine houses and settle down, and when your herds and flocks grow large and your silver and gold increase and all you have is multiplied, then your heart will become proud and you will forget the Lord your God.

Deuteronomy 8:11–14

"When you give a banquet, invite the poor, the crippled, the lame, the blind, and you will be blessed. Although they cannot repay you, you will be repaid at the resurrection of the righteous."

Luke 14:13–14

*Devotional Thought on*
# VALUES

S ome guidelines are absolute. The Ten Commandments, for example, never change. It is never right to commit adultery, murder someone, or love anything more than you love God. But other things are more like keys on a piano. The notes are not right or wrong by themselves; it depends on how they're played within a song.

For example, fighting seems like a bad thing. But throughout the Bible, God allows fighting to protect one's family or one's country. Compassion is considered a good thing, yet at times we must put our feelings aside to see that justice is not ignored.

With God's wisdom and good counsel from godly people, we can learn to do the right thing when the line between right and wrong is not clear. Solomon said, "The beginning of wisdom is this: Get wisdom. Though it cost all you have, get understanding" (Proverbs 4:7). This comes only from God.

# God's Words of Life on
# WISDOM

If you call out for insight
   and cry aloud for understanding,
and if you look for it as for silver
   and search for it as for hidden treasure,
then you will understand the fear of the Lord
   and find the knowledge of God.
For the Lord gives wisdom;
      from his mouth come knowledge and
      understanding.

PROVERBS 2:3–6

"The fear of the Lord—that is wisdom,
   and to shun evil is understanding."

JOB 28:28

Trust in the Lord with all your heart
   and lean not on your own understanding;
in all your ways submit to him,
   and he will make your paths straight.

PROVERBS 3:5–6

"Everyone who hears these words of mine and puts them into practice is like a wise man who built his house on the rock. The rain came down, the streams rose, and the winds blew and beat against that house; yet it did not fall, because it had its foundation on the rock."

MATTHEW 7:24–25

Do you not know?
    Have you not heard?
The LORD is the everlasting God,
    the Creator of the ends of the earth.
He will not grow tired or weary,
    and his understanding no one can fathom.
He gives strength to the weary
    and increases the power of the weak.

ISAIAH 40:28–29

Whether you turn to the right or to the left, your ears will hear a voice behind you, saying, "This is the way; walk in it."

ISAIAH 30:21

The wisdom that comes from heaven is first of all pure; then peace-loving, considerate, submissive, full of mercy and good fruit, impartial and sincere.

JAMES 3:17

Get wisdom, get understanding. . . .

Do not forsake wisdom, and she will protect you;
    love her, and she will watch over you.

The beginning of wisdom is this: Get wisdom.
    Though it cost all you have, get understanding.

PROVERBS 4:5–7

Where then does wisdom come from?
    Where does understanding dwell?

It is hidden from the eyes of every living thing,
    concealed even from the birds of the sky. . . .

God understands the way to it
    and he alone knows where it dwells.

JOB 28:20–21, 23

The foolishness of God is wiser than human wisdom, and the weakness of God is stronger than human strength.

1 CORINTHIANS 1:25

[Wisdom calls,] "Whoever listens to me
    will live in safety
and be at ease, without fear of harm."

PROVERBS 1:33

If any of you lacks wisdom, you should ask God, who gives generously to all without finding fault, and it will be given to you.

JAMES 1:5

*Devotional Thought on*

# WISDOM

Solomon will forever be remembered as Israel's wisest king. And, no doubt, he would have bragged about how bright his children were as well. But wise old Solomon didn't leave anything to chance; he didn't just figure that his children would pick up this wisdom on their own.

The book of Proverbs is actually a love note to Solomon's children. Wise and wealthy as he was, Solomon took the time to pour this wisdom into his children. As a result of his efforts, men and women throughout history have basked in the glow of these wise words.

Do you wonder where Solomon got the idea to give this wisdom to his children himself? How did he figure out that they needed actual instruction?

David told his son just before his own death, "Be strong, act like a man, and observe what the LORD your God requires" (1 Kings 2:2–3). *What a good idea*, Solomon must have thought as he shuffled off to his bedroom. *When I have children of my own, I think I'll do the same.*

Like father, like son.

# God's Words of Life on
# WORK

When God gives someone wealth and possessions,
and the ability to enjoy them, to accept their lot
and be happy in their toil—this is a gift of God.

ECCLESIASTES 5:19

Always give yourselves fully to the work of the Lord,
because you know that your labor in the Lord is not in vain.

1 CORINTHIANS 15:58

Whatever your hand finds to do, do it with all your might.

ECCLESIASTES 9:10

"I know your deeds, your hard work and your
perseverance. . . . You have persevered and have endured
hardships for my name, and have not grown weary."

REVELATION 2:2–3

Whatever you do, work at it with all your heart, as working
for the Lord, not for human masters, since you know that
you will receive an inheritance from the Lord as a reward.

COLOSSIANS 3:23–24

All hard work brings a profit.

PROVERBS 14:23


May the favor of the Lord our God rest on us;
establish the work of our hands for us.

PSALM 90:17


Be strong and do not give up, for your work will be
rewarded.

2 CHRONICLES 15:7


The LORD will open the heavens, the storehouse of his
bounty, to send rain on your land in season and to bless
all the work of your hands.

DEUTERONOMY 28:12


For six days, work is to be done, but the seventh day
shall be your holy day, a day of sabbath rest to the LORD.

EXODUS 35:2


The desires of the diligent are fully satisfied.

PROVERBS 13:4


The plans of the diligent lead to profit
as surely as haste leads to poverty.

PROVERBS 21:5

Sow your seed in the morning,
> and at evening let not your hands not be idle,
for you do not know which will succeed,
> whether this or that,
> or whether both will do equally well.

ECCLESIASTES 11:6

Make it your ambition to lead a quiet life: You should mind your own business and work with your hands, . . . so that your daily life may win the respect of outsiders and so that you will not be dependent on anybody.

1 THESSALONIANS 4:11–12

"Well done, good and faithful servant! You have been faithful with a few things; I will put you in charge of many things. Come and share your master's happiness!"

MATTHEW 25:21

## Devotional Thought on
# WORK

King Solomon provides us with an employment choice: "You can trade the sweat and toil behind door number two for the box that Johnny is bringing down the aisle right now."

"I'll take the box," we say without thinking. "Purposeless work is not for me."

As Solomon lifts the top off the box, we hear these words: "Each of them may eat and drink, and find satisfaction in all their toil—this is the gift of God" (Ecclesiastes 3:13). Did you hear that? Work is not a curse. Work is a blessing.

You spend more of your waking hours engaged in work than in any other activity. Can you imagine that your gracious heavenly Father, the One who has given you life and who lovingly sustains it, would want you to dread the largest slice of your life? Not a chance.

Carefully examine what you're doing with your work. Is the work of your hands satisfying to you? Do you feel God's blessing on your labor? If the answer is yes to these questions, you've got something to be thankful for. If it's no, this may be a good time to make a thorough evaluation of your job.

# Scripture Index